BART ARDIJNS

40 amazing desserts

PHOTOGRAPHY KRIS VLEGELS

LANNOO

BART ARDIJNS

Dear Reader,

A year ago, I had my very first appointment with Lannoo publishers. Since then I've worked hard, and with lots of enthusiasm, to give optimal shape to the proposed concept.
The result is a professional edition of 'desserts', presented on the plate, with an emphasis on variety of colours, flavours, textures, ingredients and techniques. In this book you will find 40 delicious desserts, from legendary classics to more exclusive creations.
I love my profession and have spent a huge amount of time developing these desserts, experimenting with different flavour combinations and forms of presentation, always with a keen sense of precision and personal touch. The visual aspect and use of high quality ingredients, supported by correctly applied techniques, are the key to a rational and successful dessert.

MY TRAINING AND MY PASSION
My passion for patisserie developed during my college training. This gave me the essential basis that I was then able to develop intensively at Relais Desserts Patisserie Wittamer in Brussels for four years. This unique work experience, combined with various courses at home and abroad, enabled me continuously to expand my knowledge and expertise in patisserie, chocolate and desserts.
For 20 years already, I have been passing on my professional knowledge to the students of the Ter Groene Poorte professional school in Bruges. At this gastronomic school, I try day by day to inspire and enthuse our future professionals in the regular lessons on patisserie and chocolate and in the special course 'individual desserts with a focus on taste and texture combinations'.

Enjoy this book to the full, let it carry you into a world of flavours, colours and shapes with attention to the very best quality.

Have as much fun using the recipes as I've had writing them!

Ingredients – *p. 6*

CHAPTER 1
BASIC PRINCIPLES & TECHNIQUES

1. Use of gelatine – *p. 17*
2. Anglaise – *p. 18*
3. Ice with desserts – *p. 18*
4. Crumble – streusel – shortbread – *p. 20*
5. Espuma – *p. 21*
6. Sponge cake – *p. 22*
7. Crémeux – *p. 23*
8. What is infusing? – *p. 23*
9. Light candying of thin slices of citrus fruit or fine strips of citrus zest – *p. 24*
10. Crispy decorations – *p. 25*
11. Caramelized puff pastry ('Inversé' or reverse processing method) – *p. 25*
12. Isomalt decoration – *p. 27*
13. Chocolate processing – *p. 28*

CHAPTER 2
ESSENTIAL CLASSICS

15 successful classic desserts that form the basis for many other creations. Where high quality raw materials and the correct techniques are used and the individual components are well balanced, it's no surprise that these desserts have become legendary!

Flan au caramel – *p. 38*
Profiterole with vanilla ice cream and chocolate sauce – *p. 40*
Elderflower and fresh fruit gratin in sabayon – *p. 42*
Moelleux au chocolat (molten chocolate cake) – *p. 44*
Brussels waffle – *p. 46*
Crème brûlée – *p. 54*
Vanilla bavarois with berries – *p. 56*
Crêpe suzette – *p. 58*
Brownie with chocolate mousse – *p. 60*
Pavlova – *p. 62*
Lemon pie – *p. 66*
Dame blanche – *p. 70*
Île flottante (floating island) – *p. 74*
Tiramisu – *p. 76*
Tarte tatin – *p. 80*

CHAPTER 3
DESSERTS WITH FRUIT AND CHOCOLATE

Personalized creations and a selection of 10 colourful summer desserts and 10 desserts where chocolate plays the leading role.

Raspberry – strawberry – almond milk – lemongrass – p. 88
Chocolate – Rodenbach – red fruits – p. 92
Yoghurt – passionfruit – mango – lime – white chocolate – p. 96
Praliné – chocolate – fruity caramel – p. 100
Wild strawberry – coconut – kaffir lime – p. 106
Chocolate flan – pear – caramel – p. 110
Mascarpone – orange – elderflower – p. 116
Chocolate – whipped cream with kirsch – slightly sour cherry – p. 120
Vanilla – red fruits – hibiscus rose hip – lemongrass – p. 124
Coconut – lychee – yuzu – white chocolate – p. 130
Pana cotta – lemon verbena – red fruit – p. 134
Spiced chocolate – orange – buckthorn – p. 138
Sour cherry clafoutis – peach – rosemary – p. 144
Tangerine – passion fruit – fruity bitter chocolate – p. 148
Beetroot – chocolate – raspberry – p. 152
Golden chocolate bar – p. 156
Lime – lemon – p. 160
Chocolate – chestnut – calamansi – p. 164
Orange – bergamot – basil – p. 170
Rhubarb – water melon – yoghurt – strawberry – p. 174

CHAPTER 4
DESSERTS FOR PERSONS WITH FOOD SENSITIVITIES

Desserts for persons with food sensitivities: 5 desserts which pay attention to gluten and/or lactose intolerance and/or in which no sugars are added.

Yoghurt – pistachio – cherry – almonds – p. 182
Tangerine – coriander – grapefruit – p. 184
Chocolate – sansho – lemon – p. 188
Pancake – chocolate – strawberries – p. 192
Blackcurrant – violet – red fruit – p. 194

———

A word of heartfelt thanks – p. 198

Ingredients

STRAWBERRIES

Deliciously sweet, juicy Belgian strawberries are well known for their superior quality and are ideal for many desserts. There are hundreds of species of strawberries, but only a few varieties (Elsanta, Darselect, Korona …) are always in our stores because they are the most suitable for sale (best mix of attractive flavour, low sensitivity to diseases and sufficient firmness for transport). Fresh strawberries can be picked from April to September. With the many different forms of cultivation, strawberries are available almost right through the year.

BERGAMOT

The bergamot is a small, round-to-pear-shaped sour citrus fruit from Bergamo in Northern Italy). The zest is lime-green, knobbly and deeply-wrinkled. The sour taste of the fruit is a cross between the lime and a bitter orange.

LEMONGRASS

Lemongrass is an Asian herb with a very fresh and lemon-like aroma and flavour. Only the first 8 to 10 cm of the stem below the top are cut into pieces and used for infusion into a liquid. Lemongrass is used mainly in Asian cuisine, but it is also very suitable for patisserie dishes to give a specific fresh citrus touch.

A brief explanation of my favourite fresh ingredients which definitely add value to a dessert. From superbly fragrant vanilla to sharp-tasting fruits used sparingly to lend greater depth.

LEMON VERBENA

The leaves of lemon verbena or verveine give off a pleasant aroma somewhere between lemon, orange and lemon grass. Lemon verbena is very tasty in a coulis or a dessert sauce, but the smaller leaves are also excellent for finishing a dessert.

KAFFIR LIME

The kaffir lime or wild lime is a small citrus fruit with little juice and a wrinkled skin that grows especially in South Asia.
In preparations it is mainly the leaves (infusions) and the zest (also known as combava) that are used. Kaffir lime gives a rather more intense and perfumed aroma than lime.

SEA BUCKTHORN

Sea buckthorn is mainly found in dunes on the Belgian, Dutch and English coasts. The plant bears bright orange berries, which are picked in late August and September. The attractively-coloured berries and the pulp have a fruity but very sour taste.

RASPBERRY

The raspberry is one of my favourite fruits, with its attractive shape and easy combination with other flavours. The plants, originating from the rose family, are native to the whole of Europe and easy to find. There are hundreds of varieties of raspberries, not only the red ones we all know but also yellow. Delicious, tender fruit to be used as quickly as possible. Raspberries are ready to pick from June to October.

HIBISCUS

The hibiscus comes from Mediterranean and tropical areas around the world. The tree has large trumpet-shaped flowers in colours ranging from white, pink, and red to purple. It's the flower's dried calyxes that are used mainly in patisserie and for other applications, ranging from tea to herbal infusions.

Hibiscus is interesting not only for its beautiful colour (rose-red) but is also very tasty thanks to its sour accent, which gives a good food pairing with red fruits and even chocolate.

CALAMANSI

This green to orange citrus fruit originates in China, but is grown widely in the Philippines, India and Malaysia. The shape of the calamansi is closest to that of a tangerine, but in taste it comes near a lime. The calamansi features a complex citrus aroma of lime, tangerine and kumquat.

RHUBARB

Rhubarb, known for its long green to red meaty stems, is always very sour to the taste; but, after adding a correct amount of sugar, is perfect for a sweet-sour dessert. Rhubarb is already available from April. When thin and softly fibrous there's no need to peel the stem. Slice the rhubarb into the desired pieces and blanch or cook in a vacuum bag with the necessary amount of sugar and possibly fresh herbs (lemon verbena). Did you know that the rhubarb is not really a fruit but a vegetable? The redder the stem, the sweeter the taste. Available from April to July.

VANILLA

Vanilla is a widely used and very welcome taste for many desserts. Originally from Mexico, vanilla sticks are the 'black gold' of the patisserie trade.

The fruits come from the climbing orchid, actually from two different climbing orchids. Most vanilla is produced from planifolia, which has a very strong vanilla aroma and flavour. The famous and high 'bourbon' quality comes mainly from Madagascar, the Comoros islands and Réunion, but also from other tropical regions such as West India.

There are also the vanilla pods of the tahitensis orchid, coming mainly from Tahiti. These are characterized by a slightly fruity, and soft and flowery aroma.

Vanilla pods are always picked unripe and green. They are first briefly immersed in hot water. After that they are slowly dried and a 'fermentation' process starts that can easily last for up to six months. During this controlled process, the black shiny vanilla sticks are formed with their very fine vanilla aroma and flavour.

CORRECT USE OF VANILLA STICKS

Hold the narrow end of the vanilla stick with the index finger and cut the entire stick down the middle with a sharp knife. Then remove the vanilla marrow with the back of the knife and add this to the preparation.

When using a liquid, you can also heat the scraped-out vanilla stick to boiling point and infuse for a few hours or overnight. In this way you arrive at a fuller, more intense vanilla flavour.

TIPS

If using a vanilla stick in a liquid, it is necessary – after infusion – to pour it through a fine sieve to separate out smaller impurities from the vanilla stick (and the stick itself) from the mass.
Dry, scraped-out vanilla sticks can still be used in two ways:
1. Place in a jar of sugar. After a while the sugar will take on the full vanilla aroma.
2. Dry the sticks completely so that they can be ground into fine vanilla powder (for use in butter dough, crumbles etc.).

ELDERFLOWER

Elderflower comes from the elder bush; You'll find these 'flower screens' with their little white flowers between May and July.

It is a very pleasant herb that has a light sweet, but also fresh taste and aroma. Very tasty in herbal infusions, but also as elderflower syrup and liqueur.

YUZU

The yuzu is a Japanese citrus fruit that at times looks a bit like a tangerine that has grown wrong. The colours can range from lime green to orange or fresh yellow. The fruit has very sour juice and a very complex aroma of spicy lemon, tangerine and lime all together. In Europe you can buy it as juice and as powder.

CHAPTER 1

BASIC PRINCIPLES & TECHNIQUES

Basic principles

The use of high quality ingredients and accurate weighing are of course a must in patisserie in order to achieve the desired result, but don't underestimate the effect of techniques and tricks of the trade, at both the cooking and the presentation stage. Knowing and using the correct techniques can make a real difference to a dessert.

In these preparing and finishing techniques, three key issues are constantly addressed:

1. Time
2. Movement
3. Temperature

In most cases, one cannot exist without the other. And the challenge is always to achieve a perfect combination of all three. Think about it, and you'll see that with any patisserie preparation these three issues play an important role in successful preparation and finishing to give the final dessert!

SOME EXAMPLES

When preparing a crème mousse, not only are correct movements and timing important in mixing everything together, but the temperature of the different ingredients also affects the texture of the final result.

For a chocolate mousse, for example, the lukewarm dough bomb (25-30°C), the hot chocolate (40°C) and the cold whipped cream (3°C) need to be mixed together. This composition will succeed with the desired texture (light, smooth, slightly creamy) only if each element is at these temperatures at the time of mixing (see chocolate mousse dessert p. 60). When preparing vanilla ice cream, not only does the correct temperature play a role in achieving an optimal binding of the yolks, but equally the way the mixture is handled (stirring, folding in, mixing) and the timing (cooling, ripening) are crucial in producing a delicious result.

For a butter dough (shortbread, crumble etc.), the ingredients mix quickly and easily into a homogeneous dough (without gluten formation) only if the butter is at the same temperature as the other raw materials (soft butter, ambient temperature).

When processing chocolate into chocolate decorations, timing and movement are required to bring the untempered chocolate to a correct processing temperature (45°C) (shrinkage, breakability and shine of the chocolate). Only then will you get the best result.

Techniques – Definitions

1. USE OF GELATINE

Personally, I prefer working with gelatine powder rather than gelatine leaves. This has two major advantages:
1. First and foremost, gelatine powder is cheaper than gelatine leaves.
2. Working with a gelatine jelly is more efficient when you have to prepare different recipes in which gelatine is used. You only need to make a mixture of gelatine powder and water once. After that, you just weigh out the required amount of soaked gelatine or gelatine powder. When converting gelatine leaf to gelatine powder (or vice versa) it is of course important that they have the same binding power (expressed in Bloom).

Both leaf gelatine and the powder gelatine absorb five times their weight in cold water. With soaked leaves, you always need to squeeze out the excess water, which is never the case with soaked gelatine powder.

FURTHER USE OF THE GELATINE MASS

Weigh out the required soaked mass and either add to the already warm ingredients (the heat of the ingredients will melt it) or first melt quickly in the microwave (40°C).

SUMMARY TABLE (CALCULATED AT A BINDING POWER OF 200 BLOOM)

LEAF GELATINE	GELATINE POWDER
1 LEAF (2 G)	12 G GELATINE JELLY (2 G POWDER + 5 PARTS COLD WATER = 10 G)
2 LEAVES (4 G)	24 G GELATINE JELLY (4 G POWDER + 5 PARTS COLD WATER = 20 G)
3 LEAVES (6 G)	36 G GELATINE JELLY (6 G POWDER + 5 PARTS COLD WATER = 20 G)
4 LEAVES (8 G)	48 G GELATINE JELLY (8 G POWDER + 5 PARTS COLD WATER = 20 G)
5 LEAVES (10 G)	60 G GELATINE JELLY (10 G POWDER + 5 PARTS COLD WATER = 20 G)
6 LEAVES (12 G)	72 G OF GELATINE JELLY
7 LEAVES (14 G)	84 G OF GELATINE JELLY
8 LEAVES (16 G)	96 G OF GELATINE JELLY
9 LEAVES (18 G)	108 G OF GELATINE JELLY
10 LEAVES (20 G)	120 G OF GELATINE JELLY

IN THIS WAY THE GELATINE JELLY CONSISTS OF ONE PART GELATINE POWDER AND 5 PARTS WATER.

2. ANGLAISE

In patisserie, we often encounter a composition known as an anglaise or crème anglaise. Why is it necessary to heat this to a very particular temperature (83°C)? The basis of an anglaise consists of a mixture of whole milk and/or cream, sugar and egg yolks. This is generally supplemented with flavours like vanilla, herbs or spices which in certain cases are infused into the liquid beforehand (see also p. 23).

Heat all the ingredients of an anglaise, stirring all the time, to 83°C. Correct temperature control is important (use a thermometer), as it is at 83°C that a smooth binding of the egg yolks is obtained (setting process). If the temperature is too high, the egg yolks will still set, but the binding will not be optimal and the yolks may separate from the liquid (= curdling).

It's a good idea to pour the resulting anglaise through a sieve for further processing.

APPLICATIONS IN THIS BOOK
- Flan au caramel p. 38
- Île flottante p. 74
- Vanilla bavaroise p. 56
- Crème of wild strawberry and raspberry p. 106

- Lightly spiced chocolate crème p. 138
- Crème of caramelized white chocolate p. 148
- Crème anglaise p. 159

3. ICE WITH DESSERTS

The use of ice (ice cream – milk ice – sorbet) is a great addition to many desserts in terms of texture, taste and temperature. Even a small 'quenelle' (or little ball) can immediately lift a tasty dessert to a higher level.

Ice cream, milk ice and sorbet are grouped for legal purposes under the common denominator of 'edible ice' and as such are subject to a number of conditions:
- Ice cream must have a fat content (animal milk fats) of at least 8%.
- Milk ice must have a fat content (animal milk fats) of at least 2.5%.
- A fruit sorbet must contain at least 25% fruit (or 15% for citrus fruits).
- Then, as a final category, you have 'water ice', for which there are no rules other than the general hygiene requirements.

APPLICATIONS IN THIS BOOK
- Moelleux au chocolat p. 44
- Profiterole p. 40
- Dame blanche p. 70
- Pavlova p. 62
- Tarte tatin p. 82
- Vanilla – red fruits – hibiscus-rose hip – lemongrass p. 124

VANILLA ICE CREAM
Ingredients
1 litre whole milk
400 g whipped cream (40%)
1 vanilla stick
235 g caster sugar
90 g glucose powder
70 g skimmed milk powder
stabilizer (ensures better stability
  and shelf life of the ice cream,
  amount dependent on the brand)
120 g egg yolks

Preparation
Mix the dry ingredients (caster sugar, glucose powder, skimmed milk powder, stabilizer). Heat the milk (60°C) along with the cut and scraped-out vanilla stick and then add the dry ingredients. Beat the egg yolks loosely, mix with some lukewarm milk and add to the whole. Continue to heat to produce an anglaise (83°C). Pass the composition immediately through a fine sieve and mix for 2 minutes (emulsifying/homogenizing).
Let the ice cream mix cool down quickly and place in the refrigerator (ripening process) for 12 hours.
Finally, churn the ice cream mix into a spoonable mass and use or store at once.

EXPLANATIONS ON THE VANILLA ICE CREAM PREPARATION PROCESSES

Stirred composition – anglaise
The heating to 83°C is necessary to obtain the optimal binding of the yolks. At this temperature the yolks bind smoothly into the mixture.

Emulsification – homogenizing
When mixing ice cream, the aim is to make the fat particles present as small and evenly distributed as possible. This gives a smooth structure and a very pleasant mouth feel.

Ripening process
This process allows the flavours to develop to the maximum. It's always advisable to cool the ice cream mix to 3°C as fast as possible and then 'ripen' it for 12 hours at this temperature. In this way the ice cream mix binds optimally.

Churning (-6 ° C to -8 ° C)
It is here that the ice gets the desired firmness. The faster the process, the smaller the ice crystals and the smoother the ice.

Basic principles & techniques

SORBET

A fruit sorbet always consists of a combination of sugar, water and fruit. To make a well-balanced sorbet it is important to produce a sorbet mix of between 28 – 32°Brix. The quantity of sugar, of course, varies from fruit to fruit (depending on the acidity).

A refractometer is used to measure the ratio between dissolved dry matter (sugar) and a liquid. These values are expressed in 'Brix'. You can adjust the Brix value of a sorbet mix: by adding water (or fruit purée) to it, you reduce the Brix value and by adding sugar syrup (32 °Baumé or 58 °Brix*) you raise the Brix value.

Baumé is a measure of the sugar density of sugar syrups (32 °Baumé represents a sugar syrup with a ratio of 45% water and 55% sugar).

The formula for convert Baumé to Brix is: Baumé value × 1.8 = Brix value

4. CRUMBLE – STREUSEL – SHORTBREAD

A crumble (also known as streusel, or shortbread) always has a butter dough (butter, sugar, flour) as a base. A crumble is personalized by additions like herbs, nuts, citrus zest, or various types of sugar.

IT IS ALWAYS PREPARED AS FOLLOWS

Mix soft, tempered butter (room temperature) with the flavourings and sugar(s). Finally fold in in the sifted flour, with the salt or herbs if desired, very lightly to produce a homogeneous dough (no gluten formation).

Roll out the dough evenly, or crumble it immediately on a baking tray and then bake at 150°C. If necessary, mix the crumble regularly during the baking process. This creates an evenly coloured and evenly baked crumble.

A not-too-high baking temperature (and a longer baking-drying time) gives a crumble that is not only dryer, but also crispier and can be stored longer.

For coloured crumbles (raspberry powder, matcha powder), it is even recommended to bake-dry at 100°C to avoid discolouration.

Tip for very good keeping quality:
Vacuum the fully cooled crumble at 99.8%

APPLICATIONS IN THIS BOOK
- Chocolate crumble p. 44
- Edible bottom of the Black Forest gâteau (crispy chocolate crumble) p. 123
- Yoghurt crumble p. 174
- Orange-hazelnut crumble p. 170
- Orange crumble p. 116
- Raspberry crumble p. 155
- Gluten-free chocolate-citrus crumble p. 188

SOME RECIPES
PISTACHIO CRUMBLE
Ingredients
100 g butter
100 g caster sugar
100 g ground pistachio
100 g flour
2 g coarse sea salt

YUZUCRUMBLE

Ingredients

100 g butter
grated zest of one 1 lemon
100 g caster sugar
90 g finely ground hazelnut powder
90 g flour
8 g yuzu powder
3 g coarse sea salt
80 g feuilletine

MATCHA TEA CRUMBLE

Ingredients

150 g butter
grated zest of 3 limes
150 g caster sugar
150 g almond powder
15 g matcha tea powder

5. ESPUMA

Literally translated, the Spanish word 'espuma' means foam or mousse. Espumas for desserts are compositions based on fruit purées (or juices), yoghurt, alcohol, herbal infusions or chocolate, sweetened as necessary and to which a quantity of N2O (nitrous oxide or 'laughing gas') is added to make the liquid composition 'more frothy' and firmer.

Preparation is relatively easy (the raw materials are always mixed homogeneously), but the firmness and smoothness of an espuma are determined by the ratio of the ingredients with the gelatine (or other binders), pasteurized protein or fat (cream) and by the amount of N2O.

In a relatively fast way, a texture and volume are created which produce an attractive added value in combination with other flavours and textures.

PROCESSING TIPS

1. Always sieve the composition into the espuma bottle/whipped cream siphon
2. Both the composition and the bottle/siphon are stored in the refrigerator (3°C).
3. Shake well before use and mix with the necessary gas (N2O) until the espuma has reached the desired firmness and smoothness.

APPLICATIONS IN THIS BOOK
- Lemongrass espuma p. 91
- Rodenbach espuma p. 95

SOME RECIPES

YOGHURT ESPUMA

Ingredients

250 g Greek yoghurt
15 g yoghurt powder
165 g cream (35%)
50 g of sugar syrup 1/1 or 30 °Baumé

ELDERFLOWER AND RASPBERRY ESPUMA

Ingredients

150 g elderflower syrup
350 g raspberry puree with 10% sugar
100 g cream (35%)
2 gelatine leaves

CHOCOLATE ESPUMA

Ingredients

200 g dark chocolate
150 g cream (35%)
150 g pasteurized egg white

YUZU AND VANILLA ESPUMA

Ingredients

150 g whole milk
½ vanilla stick
35 g caster sugar
50 g yuzu purée 100%
2 gelatine leaves
150 g cream (35%)

6. SPONGE CAKE

The technique consists of making a mixture of the basic ingredients, combining with N2O (= 'laughing gas') under pressure (using an espuma bottle or a whipped cream siphon) and then 'cooking' in a microwave oven. In this way a lightweight cake structure is obtained very quickly. With a proper distribution of the gas in the mixture and a correct 'cooking' time, one achieves a cake structure comparable with that of a sponge. Many flavouring, colour and aroma combinations are possible, but one has to get the preparation right:

1. Weigh the ingredients correctly and mix homogeneously (mix everything together smoothly with the Thermomix).
2. Rub the resulting mass through a round-bottomed sieve to avoid blockage of the membrane (in the espuma bottle/whipped cream siphon).
3. Mix the mass well (shake well) with the N2O added into the bottle and fill the insulated foam beakers just half way. Insulated foam beakers do not melt and are a perfect insulator during the cooking process. They also protect the resulting very airy structure from drying out.
4. As a last step, the sponge cakes are cooked one by one in the microwave for 20-30 seconds at high power (depending on the microwave power). Immediately turn them upside down onto baking paper to prevent them from drying out. Cut the sponge cake from the wall and remove from the mould when needed.

STORAGE TIP
Once the sponge cakes have cooled, place them immediately, along with the insulated beakers, in a fully sealed plastic bag. Close the bag airtight with a zipper or seal it.

APPLICATIONS IN THE BOOK
- Pistachio sponge cake p. 127
- Vanilla sponge cake p. 163
- Chocolate sponge cake p. 123
- Hazelnut crumble p. 110
- Red beet sponge cake p. 155

SOME RECIPES

SPONGE CAKE WITH YOGHURT AND BASIL

Ingredients

200 g pasteurized egg white
40 g almond powder
40 g yoghurt powder
45 g caster sugar
15 g flour
7 g fresh basil
grated zest of ⅓ lime

SPONGE CAKE WITH RASPBERRIES

Ingredients

165 g eggs
60 g egg yolks
105 g icing sugar
30 g almond powder
60 g flour
30 g raspberry powder

 Scan the QR code or go to www.lannoopublishinggroup.com/desserts-video-en

7. CRÉMEUX

A crémeux always has an anglaise as a base (see explanation of an anglaise on p. 18). Afterwards, a binder (gelatine) is added and, lastly, the soft butter is folded in at 38°C to achieve a homogeneous smooth crème, or 'crémeux'. A crémeux always has a smooth texture and a beautiful shine as the final result.

APPLICATIONS IN THE BOOK
- Raspberry and black currant (cassis) crémeux p. 127
- Passion fruit crémeux p. 96
- Lemon and lime crémeux p. 160
- Lime and kaffir lime crémeux p. 109
- Bergamot-basil crémeux p. 170
- Orange crémeux p. 170
- Sour cherry (griotte) crémeux p. 92
- Calamansi crémeux p. 167
- Tangerine crémeux p. 151

8. WHAT IS INFUSING?

Infusing consists of allowing flavours to enter into liquids, such as a vanilla stick into a cream preparation, or tea or spices into hot water ... The dosage depends on the ingredient and the ratio to the totality of the ingredients.
Always pass an infusion through a fine sieve before continuing the preparation.

APPLICATIONS IN THE BOOK
- Hibiscus-rose hip and lemongrass syrup p. 124
- White chocolate-mascarpone panna-cotta p. 134
- Lime-kaffir lime crémeux p. 109
- Orange coulis see p. 58

WHAT IS VACUUM INFUSING?
A vacuum machine is used for manipulating flavour combinations and structures, for example in fruit. When fruit is vacuumed with a liquid (syrup, coulis ...) at the appropriate pressure, the fruit not only swells slightly but also the cell walls burst lightly. The added fluid can then penetrate much more easily into the cell walls. This allows them to be saturated with the added liquid. The fluid-syrup infusion is, as it were, impregnated into the fruit.

APPLICATION IN THE BOOK
- Lightly candied lime particles in syrup p. 160

9. LIGHT CANDYING OF THIN SLICES OF CITRUS FRUIT OR FINE STRIPS OF CITRUS ZEST (ORANGE, LIME, BERGAMOT, LEMON ETC.)

Candying consists of saturating the portions of citrus fruit or of citrus fruit zest with sugar, not only to make the zest edible and decorative when placing the dessert on the plate, but also to extend the shelf life of fruit and zest considerably. Note: fruit slices and zest need to be candied separately.

TECHNOLOGY
Wash and dry the citrus fruits thoroughly before removing a fine zest. This zest may already be cut into fine strips. Dip (blanch) the citrus fruit slices/strips of zest into hot (non-boiling), lightly salted water. Then rinse with cold water. Repeat this step twice in fresh water; this treatment removes the bitterness of the skin and also modifies its cell structure, making it more porous and much more able to absorb the sugar (candying).

Following this preparation, follow the various steps of candying:

Bring a thin sugar syrup (26 °Baumé (*)) slowly to the boil. That is, a sugar solution of 275 g water and 225 g caster sugar, i.e. 55% water and 45% sugar. Then add the citrus fruit slices/ strips of zest.

Leave the sugar syrup with the citrus fruit/zest to cool for 24 hours at room temperature.

To optimize the candying process, remove the fruit or zest and allow excess sugar to drip off, and then add 50 g of sugar to the sugar syrup. Bring to the boil slowly again, take the pot off the heat and add the fruit/zest. Leave to cool again to room temperature. Repeat these steps until the desired degree of 'candying' (from lightly to heavily) is achieved.

APPLICATION IN THE BOOK
Lightly candied orange strips see p. 58

WHAT IS A BAUMÉ METER? (*)
A Baumé meter is a sugar thickness meter, that is an instrument that measures the amount of sugar in a sugar solution.
Some ratios (measured at 18°C):
- 25 °Baumé represents a ratio of 60% water and 40% caster sugar
- 26 °Baumé represents a ratio of 55% water and 45% caster sugar
- 30 °Baumé represents a ratio of 50% water and 50 % caster sugar
- 32 °Baumé represents a ratio of 45% water and 55% caster sugar
- 35 °Baumé represents a ratio of 40% water and 60% caster sugar

WHAT IS A REFRACTOMETER?
A refractometer is used to measure the ratio between dissolved dry matter (sugar) and a liquid. These values are expressed in 'Brix' (See Ice with desserts on p. 18).
Baumé values are converted to Brix values using the formula: Baumé value × 1.8 = Brix value.

10. CRISPY DECORATIONS
Drying technique
Drying consists of removing moisture from a product by circulating heat and air around it (drying tower). This technique used to be used to give foodstuffs a longer shelf life. Today, drying is mainly used to give desserts an extra dimension (crispy decoration). In addition, drying contributes to a more intense taste.

APPLICATIONS IN THE BOOK
- Hibiscus meringues p. 128
- Passionfruit foam p. 99
- Rhubarb snippets p. 174
- Strawberry-raspberry croquant p. 177
- Blueberry meringue rods p. 141
- Sugar-free meringues (cooking foam) p. 184
- Violet and blackcurrant croquant p. 194

 Scan the QR code or go to www.lannoopublishinggroup.com/desserts-video-en

11. CARAMELIZED PUFF PASTRY ('INVERSÉ' OR REVERSE PROCESSING METHOD)

This puff pastry consists of a reversed operation. For normal pastry, the butter is mixed directly into the dough. In puff pastry, the butter (with flour mixed in) is placed around the dough and then rolled in (see below) to give several thin inter-leaved layers of dough and butter (in French 'tourer').

The reverse or 'inversé' method has several advantages:
- smoother rolling, less rapid gluten formation
- less susceptible to shrinkage during baking
- better puffing after baking
- more pronounced butter flavour of the puff pastry

BUTTER-FLOUR MIX
Ingredients
535 g butter (85% butterfat)
215 g flour

Preparation
Cut the cold butter into smallish pieces and mix with the flour in a mixer fitted with a dough hook at low speed into a homogeneous dough.
Roll the resulting dough evenly into a rectangle between baking paper sheets,

Basic principles & techniques

cover with plastic and leave to cool for an hour in the refrigerator.

PRE-DOUGH
Ingredients
500 g flour
18 g salt
160 g butter (85% butterfat)
215 g of hot water
5 g vinegar

Preparation
Fold all the ingredients into a homogeneous dough in a mixer with a dough hook.
Roll the resulting dough evenly to half the size of the butter-flour mix and also leave covered for an hour in the refrigerator.

ROLLING PUFF PASTRY (*TOURER*)
Place the rolled out pre-dough mix on top of the butter dough mix, and fold over the butter dough mix to cover it (i.e. with the butter-flour mix on the outside). Roll out together into a rectangular shape with a uniform thickness of 1 cm.
Then fold into four (double folding).
Cover and leave for an hour in the refrigerator.
Fold in four a second time.
Cover and leave for an hour in the refrigerator.
Then fold into three (simple folding).
Roll the puff pastry out a last time to 3 mm thick and leave for a few hours in the refrigerator.

APPLICATION THE BOOK
- Tarte tatin, p. 80

BART'S TIPS
Adding vinegar to the pre-dough gives the puff pastry a longer refrigerator shelf life.
Make sure that the pre-dough and the butter-flour mix are both at the same cool temperature and suppleness when rolling out.
Leave for sufficient time to rest between the different rolling out stages and before finally cutting the rolled-out puff pastry.
Always make sure that you have an even 1 cm thickness when rolling out.

12. ISOMALT DECORATION

Isomalt (decoration used for desserts on p. 109 and p. 192).

For decorations on desserts, isomalt is used mainly in place of the classic water – caster sugar – glucose mix. Why?
Isomalt is easier and faster to use, there is no need to weigh it out, and the decorations, once made, are less sensitive to moisture absorption (much easier both to prepare and store).

TECHNIQUE
Melt the isomalt slowly, without adding water. Once everything is melted, boil to 150 to 165°C to stiffen. The higher the cooking temperature, the shinier, the firmer and less moisture-sensitive the result, but also the more difficult to process (need to act more quickly).

Note: If you want to colour the isomalt, do so at 130°C using water-based colourings.
When the isomalt reaches the desired temperature, pour it onto a silicone mat; by regularly folding the edges of the isomalt inwards (using a silicone mat), a cooler, workable isomalt mass is produced.
Now satinate the isomalt. Put on suitable gloves (for sugar processing), pull out the mass and fold it back repeatedly. During this process, the isomalt changes colour and the shine is created.
From now on keep the temperature of the isomalt stable by holding it under a sugar lamp. If you want to heat it lightly, this is best done in a microwave oven, briefly, on a small silicone mat.
For irregular-shaped isomalt rings, draw out one end of the mass thinly but evenly and lay it round a biscuit cutter of the desired diameter. Cut the end of the still soft isomalt with good scissors. Always store isomalt decorations in a well-sealed box, with layers of baking paper between the decorations and with moisture adsorption bags.

13. CHOCOLATE PROCESSING

With pre-crystallized chocolate and some simple techniques, a dessert can be raised to a higher level with a nice, rational, chocolate decoration.
To achieve the desired result, there are some important points you need to bear in mind when working the chocolate.

MELTING

Always melt the chocolate at 45°C. This ensures that all crystal forms (present in the cocoa butter) are fully melted. This can be done in various ways:

- **in the microwave**
Heat the chocolate in brief steps in the microwave (medium power) and mix well before heating further. Make sure the chocolate does not burn;

- **in the chocolate melter**
Place the chocolate overnight in the melter at 45°C;

- **with a tempering machine**
Melt the chocolate beforehand with a tempering machine: there exist small and very practical table tempering machines for the catering industry.

PRE-CRYSTALLIZING

The purpose of pre-crystallization is to create stable crystal shapes in the chocolate. With the right crystal structure, you will end up with a shiny chocolate with a certain hardness and the required shrinkage potential.
It is not important which method you prefer for crystallizing the chocolate, but always the same parameters are vital: time, movement and temperature.
It is also necessary to mix the chocolate optimally before starting the pre-crystallization process.

Traditional pre-crystallization method

Pour two-thirds of the well-blended chocolate (45°C) onto a very clean marble plate. Allow the mass to cool by constantly moving the chocolate with a pointed palette knife. When the chocolate becomes slightly thicker (more viscous), it is time to mix this well with the remaining (⅓) of the chocolate at 45°C.

More modern pre-crystallization method (grafting method)

In this method, small pieces of hard chocolate (callets) are added to the molten chocolate mass (45°C) and stirred very well, with the aim of lowering the temperature to the desired processing temperature.

CHECK THE CHOCOLATE FOR FURTHER PROCESSING AFTER CORRECT PRE-CRYSTALLIZATION

Each chocolate has its target temperature for optimal results (white chocolate 28-29°C, milk chocolate 29-30°C, dark chocolate 31-32°C), but this does not mean that the correct crystal shape is always achieved.
A much more efficient method is to take a chocolate 'sample' on the corner of a (palette) knife; if the correct crystal shapes have been reached, the chocolate will be completely hard after 3-5 minutes and show a slight shine at 18-20°C. This is the most correct confirmation that the chocolate is ready for further processing.
If necessary, you can still warm the chocolate indirectly, either in a microwave oven or using a heat gun.

STORING OF CHOCOLATE DECORATIONS

Chocolate should always be kept in an airtight container (away from other odours, light and moisture). Store it at a stable temperature of 12-18°C (not refrigerator!). Remove the plastic from the chocolate decorations only when you really need them.

TECHNIQUE FOR THE CHOCOLATE DECORATIONS GIVEN IN THIS BOOK

Thin chocolate spears
- Moelleux au chocolat p. 44
- Profiterole with vanilla ice cream and chocolate sauce p. 40
- Chocolate-whipped cream with kirsch-slightly sour cherry p. 120

Spread the pre-crystallized chocolate thinly on a marble leaf and make quick, short movements from left to right with a fillet knife.

Circular net – dreamcatcher in chocolate
- Dame blanche p. 70

Using a finely snipped-off icing bag, make a circle of the desired size on baking paper, and then fill in immediately with other circular lines. Once crystallization starts, remove the excess chocolate (chocolate lines outside of the circle).

Moon-shaped chocolate decoration
- Lime – lemon p. 160

Pre-mix white liquid chocolate with powder colouring (fat-soluble) to the desired green colour and then pre-crystallize correctly.

Using an icing bag, produce lines on a cold metal pipe (deep freezer) of the desired diameter; then remove the chocolate decoration from the pipe at once with a palette knife.

 Scan the QR code or go to www.lannoopublishinggroup.com/desserts-video-en

Red chocolate ribbon
- Clafoutis of sour cherry – peach – rosemary p. 144

Mix the melted cocoa butter with the red powder colouring (fat-soluble) and mix both homogeneously.
After the coloured cocoa butter has pre-crystallized, brush it onto a plastic ribbon of the desired size using a brush or sponge. Once the cocoa butter has crystallized, immediately apply a layer of pre-crystallized white chocolate on top. Bend the plastic ribbon to the desired diameter. Allow to dry completely and remove the plastic only just before use.

Parallel chocolate circles
- Orange – bergamot – basil p. 170

Apply a small quantity of pre-crystallized dark chocolate onto a plastic ribbon and "comb" it to create fine, separate, parallel lines. Connect these lines directly. This is done using a one-way icing bag with a finely snipped-off end to decorate diagonal lines in the chocolate. Immediately fold the plastic ribbon into a circle and remove the plastic only just before use.

 Scan the QR code or go to www.lannoopublishinggroup.com/desserts-video-en

White chocolate with orange zest (orange crunch)
- Mascarpone – orange – elderflower p. 116

Add a mix of pre-crystallized white chocolate with orange zest to rice crispies and roll out immediately between two sheets of baking paper. Allow to harden completely and break into the desired pieces only just before use.

Transparent chocolate cylinder
• Chocolate – Rodenbach – red fruit p. 92

Using a one-way piping bag with a finely-snipped off end, place thin inter-lacing lines of pre-crystallized milk chocolate onto a square plastic sheet. Before the chocolate is fully crystallized, roll this onto a smooth cylinder. Stick the ends together with a small sticker. Leave to dry totally and remove the plastic only on use.

 Scan the QR code or go to www.lannoopublishinggroup.com/desserts-video-en

Pink chocolate tunnel
• Coconut – lychee – yuzu – white chocolate p. 130

Spread pre-crystallized white chocolate thinly onto a rectangular plastic sheet, cut to the desired size. When half-hardened, place the chocolate tightly around a PVC tube covered with a layer of baking paper. Remove the PVC tube upon full crystallization and make some holes in the chocolate tunnel with lightly heated cutters. Spray with spray chocolate in the desired colour (50% chocolate mixed with 50% cocoa butter and powder colouring as desired).

Chocolate circles
• Chocolate – whipped cream with kirsch-slightly sour cherry p. 120

Apply a quantity of pre-crystallized milk chocolate to a thin piece of plastic. Place a piece of plastic of the same size on top. With a plastic rolling pin, spread the chocolate thinly between the plastic layers. Once the chocolate has reached the desired crystallization-hardness, cut out the required circles without removing the plastic. Leave to dry totally and remove the plastic only on use.

 Scan the QR code or go to www.lannoopublishinggroup.com/desserts-video-en

Basic principles & techniques /// 31

Coloured chocolate curl

• Chocolate – chestnut – calamansi p. 164

Using a brush or sponge, apply pre-crystallized and coloured cocoa butter (red) thinly onto a plastic ribbon. When sufficiently hardened, apply a thin layer of pre-crystallized white chocolate on top. When this feels 'dry', spread a final thin layer of fondant chocolate on top. Cut into wedge-shaped triangles and fold into a circular pie ring until complete crystallization. Leave to dry totally and remove the plastic only on use.

White chocolate and rice crispie circles

• Tangerine – passion fruit – chocolate 64% p. 148

Mix a little pre-crystallized white chocolate with rice crispies and roll out immediately between two sheets of baking paper. When half-hardened, remove one side of the baking paper. Cut out circles as desired.

Dark chocolate loopings

• Chocolate gold bar p. 156

Apply pre-crystallized dark chocolate to a plastic strip and comb with a silicone comb to create even chocolate lines. Once the chocolate is half-crystallized-hardened, fold the plastic strip with the chocolate once round the thumb. Leave to dry totally and remove the plastic only on use.

Chocolate fan
- Praliné – chocolate – fruity caramel p. 100

Mix milk chocolate (40°C) with 5% neutral oil (grape seed oil) and spread out very thin on a clean marble block. Once the chocolate has hardened sufficiently, cut out your fans with a sharp-pointed knife.

Thin chocolate slices
- Praliné – chocolate – fruity caramel p. 100

Spread the pre-crystallized dark chocolate thinly onto a plastic sheet. Once half-crystallized, cut out slices with a paring knife. Leave to dry totally and remove the plastic only on use.

Coloured chocolate circles
- Spicy chocolate – orange – sea buckthorns p. 138

With a fine sponge, apply a layer of yellow-coloured, pre-crystallized cocoa butter on plastic, and then a fine layer of red-coloured pre-crystallized cocoa butter. Finally add a thin layer of pre-crystallized fondant chocolate. Cut out immediately to the desired diameter.

Basic principles & techniques

CHAPTER 2

ESSENTIAL CLASSICS

Flan au caramel

*An easily prepared vanilla flan,
combined with caramel sauce running off onto the plate ...*

FLAN

Ingredients
300 ml whole milk
150 g cream (35%)
½ vanilla stick
150 g egg yolks
75 g caster sugar
54 g gelatine (or 4 ½ gelatine leaves)

Preparation
Mix the milk and cream together with the scraped-out vanilla stick and heat to around 50°C. Add a portion of the warm milk-cream-vanilla mixture to the loosely beaten yolks and the caster sugar. Then mix and heat, stirring all the time, to 83°C to produce an anglaise. Pour immediately through a fine sieve and add the soaked and squeezed gelatine. Allow to cool to 30°C, stirring regularly. Fill the desired moulds (little plastic pots or silicon baking moulds) with the mixture and leave to cool in the refrigerator (3°C) for at least 6 hours.

CARAMEL SAUCE

Ingredients
60 g glucose
200 g caster sugar
180 g water

Preparation
Heat the glucose with the caster sugar on a low flame and allow to caramelize evenly. Quench immediately with hot water (boiling point) as soon as an attractive caramel colour develops*. Pour through a fine sieve and allow to cool completely before use.

Quenching is aimed at stopping the colour changing (caramelization) by adding hot liquid (little by little) to the caramel (mix well!).

CARAMEL DECORATION

Ingredients
80 g water
50 g glucose
250 g caster sugar

Preparation
Heat the water with the glucose and gradually add the caster sugar until the desired caramel (160-165°C) is obtained. Place the bottom of the caramel pot briefly in cold water ('scaring') to keep the caramel colour and temperature stable.
Pour onto baking paper or a silicone baking mat and create an abstract sugar decoration by making rotating movements with a fork in the slightly chilled caramel.
Leave to cool completely and then break into pieces as decoration.

NOTE
Isomalt sugar can also be used – let it melt very slowly (without additives) and caramelize. Isomalt sugar is much less sensitive to moisture.

COMPOSING THE DESSERT

Take the flans out of the moulds onto a plate or into a small bowl, add the caramel sauce to the top (running off) and decorate with the abstract caramel decoration.

BART'S TIPS

More information on the anglaise composition can be found on p. 18.

With silicone baking moulds, the flans come free more easily after a few minutes in the freezer. Afterwards, give them time to reach the desired temperature.

You can also combine this dessert with fresh fruit. Recommended.

Essential classics /// 39

Profiterole with vanilla ice cream and chocolate sauce

Delicious chocolate crispy puffs filled with creamy vanilla ice cream and a dark chocolate sauce.

PUFF BATTER

Ingredients
250 g water
125 g butter
2 g salt
2 g caster sugar
190 g flour
250-300 g eggs

Preparation
Bring the water gently to the boil with the butter, salt and sugar. Boil for 10 seconds and immediately add all the flour through a sieve (away from the heat). Mix thoroughly. Add the eggs to the batter one by one, mix vigorously with the beater spatula and check the firmness: the batter must shine and fall from the spatula in one lump.
Place puffs of the desired size on lightly greased baking plates, glaze with lightly beaten egg mixture and add a thin layer of chocolate-butter dough.
Bake the puffs at 190°C for about 18 minutes with open steam vent (baking time depends on the size of the puffs).

CHOCOLATE-BUTTER DOUGH

Ingredients
125 g butter
160 g caster sugar
145 g flour
15 g cocoa powder
2 g salt

Preparation
Mix the soft butter with the caster sugar, then add the sifted mixture of flour, cocoa powder and salt. Mix briefly into a homogeneous dough. Chill to 3°C for further processing.
Roll out the chilled dough very thin (2 mm) and press out circles of the same diameter as the puffs. Press these lightly onto tops of the puffs.
Finish baking at 190°C for about 18 minutes with open steam vent (baking time depending on the size of the puffs).

VANILLA ICE CREAM

Ingredients and preparation p. 19.

CHOCOLATE SAUCE

Ingredients
250 g whole milk
250 g cream (35%)
300 g fondant chocolate

Preparation
Heat the milk and cream together to 60°C and add step by step to the fondant chocolate. Mix regularly until the chocolate is completely absorbed into the mass.
Lastly, mix into an emulsion (homogeneous mass).

FINISHING

Chocolate stick: See chocolate techniques on p. 29

BART'S TIPS

Add the eggs one at a time and regularly check the solidity of the batter. It is quite possible that the ideal consistency will be achieved without using all the eggs.

Sugar icing on the puffs is not essential but makes them more inviting and crisper in the mouth.

More information on ice cream making terminology can be found on pp. 18–19.

Elderflower and fresh fruit gratin in sabayon

A variation on the tasty classic of sabayon with white wine by combining with an assortment of fresh fruits and an accent of elderflower liqueur. Lightly gratinated and served hot!

SABAYON

Ingredients
200 g egg yolks
90 g caster sugar
40 g elderflower liqueur
200 g cream (35%)

Preparation
Beat the egg yolks with the caster sugar and elderflower liqueur over a low heat until slightly foamy. Leave to cool slightly and then fold in the half-whipped cream.
Arrange an assortment of fruit in deep plates and pour the sabayon in between. Gratinate the top of the dessert to allow the sugars to caramelize slightly.

FINISHING
Finish with lime zest and accent of wheatgrass.

Moelleux au chocolat (molten chocolate cake)

A delicious molten chocolate cake with a hot, slightly liquid chocolate filling,
crispy chocolate crumble and refreshing vanilla ice cream!

MOELLEUX BATTER

Ingredients
100 g fondant chocolate
90 g butter
150 g eggs
100 g caster sugar
80 g flour

Preparation
Mix the fondant chocolate and the butter (40°C).
Beat the eggs with the sugar into a light, fluffy mixture and blend with the butter-fondant chocolate mixture. Lastly, fold in the sifted flour with a spatula.
Line the selected baking rings with a layer of baking paper, fill half-way and press in a ganache pearl just before baking.
Finish baking at 190°C for 10-12 minutes, depending on the volume of the moelleux.

GANACHE PEARL

Ingredients
150 g cream (35%)
45 g glucose
50 g caster sugar
175 g dark chocolate callets
40 g butter

Preparation
Bring the cream and glucose to the boil together and gradually add the dark chocolate callets. Once heated to 38°C, add the softened butter and mix everything homogeneously into an emulsion (ganache).
Pipe into a 3D ball-shaped silicone baking mat of the desired diameter and freeze for further use.

VANILLA ICE CREAM
Ingredients and preparation p. 19.

CHOCOLATE CRUMBLE

Ingredients
100 g butter
100 g caster sugar
100 g almond powder 100%
90 g flour
15 g cocoa powder
1.5 g coarse sea salt

Preparation
Mix the butter (at room temperature) with the caster sugar and almond powder.
Fold in the sieved flour, cocoa powder and coarse sea salt to produce a homogeneous dough.
Bake at 150°C. During baking, mix the crumble to produce an optimum and evenly baked result.
Allow to cool completely before cutting to fine crumble.

FINISHING
Abstract line of hazelnut (1/1) and chocolate stick (for chocolate techniques, see p. 29)

BART'S TIPS

Getting the baking time right is of decisive importance for the end result of the moelleux.

Brussels waffle

Our Belgian pride, a freshly baked yeast waffle with the typical deep, square indentations (6 × 4). Served with cream and strawberries, this is a pearl of a dessert!

WAFFLE BATTER

Ingredients
25 g fresh yeast
375 g warm water
500 g whole milk
1 vanilla stick
100 g egg yolks
500 g flour
3 g salt
300 g melted butter
150 g egg white
10 g caster sugar

Preparation
Dissolve the fresh yeast in the warm water (40°C) and add this to the whole milk with the scraped-out vanilla stick. Blend in the loosely-beaten egg yolks, followed by the sifted mixture of flour and salt. Lastly, mix in the melted butter (40°C) to give an attractive homogeneous whole. Cover this batter and leave overnight in the refrigerator at 3°C. Just before baking, stir again the 'yeasted' batter. Then beat the eggwhites with a very little sugar into a frothy liquid and stir into the batter. Place the batter in a preheated waffle iron and cook at a temperature of 200 to 220°C. Serve immediately.

ACCENT OF STRAWBERRY AND RASPBERRY CRÈME (BALL)

Ingredients
140 g whole milk
100 g egg yolks
85 g caster sugar
3 ½ gelatine leaves
105 g fresh strawberries
105 g fresh raspberries
210 g cream (35%)

Preparation
Pre-soak the gelatine. Make an anglaise (83°C) with the first three ingredients and add, using a fine sieve, to the soaked gelatine. Once you have an optimal gelatine mixture, add the strawberries and raspberries. At a temperature of 25°C, whip the cream and stir in 2/3 of it to produce a homogeneous creamy mix. Spoon the cream into a 3D ball silicone mat of the desired size and freeze. Remove from the freezer and glaze the cream balls with a neutral glaze with 15-20% raspberry purée added along with a few drops of red liquid colouring. Heat to 50°C and place a thin layer of glaze around the crémeux.
Prepare the glazed crème in a dish and combine with pieces of fresh strawberries and raspberries. Garnish with a raspberry angel and atsina cress.

RASPBERRY GEL

Ingredients
250 g raspberry purée with
    10% sugar
70 g sugar water 1/1 or 30 °Baumé
2.5 g agar agar

Preparation
Boil the raspberry purée with the sugar water and agar agar, pass through a fine sieve and allow to completely cool/solidify. Mix before use into a shiny, smooth gel, eventually passing it through a very fine sieve.

CREAM SPIRAL

Ingredients
500 g cream (35%)
45 g caster sugar

Preparation
Beat the cream with the caster sugar at medium speed into a firm but smooth, pipeable cream. Using a toothed nozzle, pipe an even spiral into a little dish.

Serve on a separate little dish with strawberry-raspberry baverois, raspberry jelly and fresh strawberries.

BART'S TIPS

More information on the anglaise composition can be found on p. 18.

Leaving the waffle batter to rest overnight brings out the flavours much better owing to the slow fermentation. Adding the whipped egg-white only afterwards improves the overall structure of the waffle (and the number of waffles).

The art of baking a Brussels waffle consists of achieving a crispy outside but a smooth, light inside.

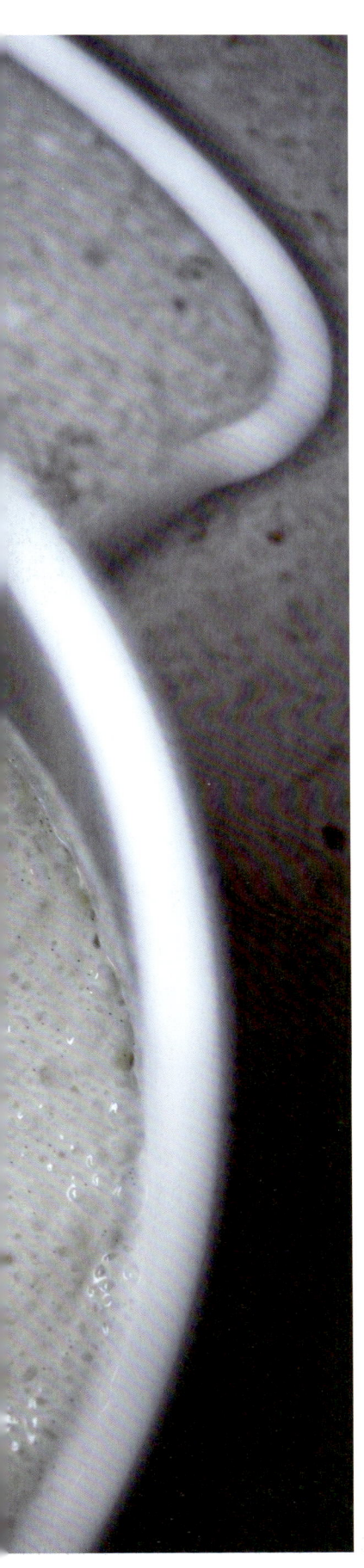

Crème brûlée

Literally translated: burned cream! A cream with a powerful, smooth texture combined with a thinly caramelized sugar layer as a 'texture breaker'.

VANILLA CREAM

Ingredients
2 vanilla sticks
500 g whipped cream (40%)
500 g whole milk
200 g egg yolks
160 g caster sugar

Preparation
Grate the vanilla sticks and add to the mixture of whipped cream and whole milk.
Add this mixture to the loosely-beaten egg yolks and caster sugar. Mix together and pour through a fine sieve.
Place the mixture in little dishes, plates or bowls and bake at 90°C for 45 to 55 minutes in a hot air oven depending on the size and volume of the crème brûlée. Check before taking out of the oven: the crème must not 'wave' but vibrate slightly if you lightly shake the baking plate.

FINISHING

Leave to cool completely, then sprinkle thinly and evenly with fine sugar. Caramelize evenly with a sufficiently powerful gas burner or a branding iron. A combination of fresh fruits is also very tasty with crème brûlée

BART'S TIPS

Getting the baking time right is essential for a sufficiently firm but unctuous structure of a crème brûlée. This can differ from oven to oven.

Vanilla bavarois with berries

A fresh vanilla bavarois with red fruit and a crispy base as texture-breaker.

CRISP BASE

Ingredients
95 g crumble (finely ground)
40 g mini rice crispies
60 g white chocolate
5 g grape seed oil
little grated lemon or lime zest

Preparation
Heat the oil and melt in the white chocolate. Then mix in together the lightly mixed crumble and the rice crispies. Add the grated lemon zest and roll out the mixture 2-3 millimetres thick, cut out to the desired diameter and chill for further use.

SOUR CHERRY COMPÔTE

Ingredients
150 g slightly chopped sour cherries (griottes)
75 g cherry juice
20 g caster sugar
0.6 g agar agar

Preparation
Bring all ingredients quickly to the boil and pour a 1 cm layer into the silicone mould. Freeze for further use.

VANILLA BAVAROIS

Ingredients
150 g cream (35%)
1 vanilla stick
40 g egg yolks
60 g caster sugar
36 g gelatine (or 3 gelatine leaves)
350 g cream (35%)

Preparation
Pre-soak the gelatine leaves. Make an anglaise with the cream, scraped-out vanilla stick, egg yolks and sugar. Place the saucepan on the stove and add the soaked gelatine. Pass through a fine sieve.
At a temperature of 28-30°C, whip the cream and stir in 2/3 of it to produce a homogeneous crème.
Fill in the selected mould (silicone mould – inverted construction) half way with the vanilla cream and press the pre-prepared sour cherry filling on top. Fill the mould to the top with the vanilla bavarois and smooth level with the edge. Cool before further use.

RASPBERRY COULIS

Ingredients
250 g raspberry purée with 10% sugar
30 g caster sugar

Preparation
Dissolve the caster sugar into the raspberry purée.

FINISHING

Glaze the vanilla bavarois moulds with the pink glaze (see also p. 109, but add white and red powder dye until the desired pink colour is obtained) and present it on the crispy base. Decorate with the white chocolate decorations, red fruit and raspberry coulis.

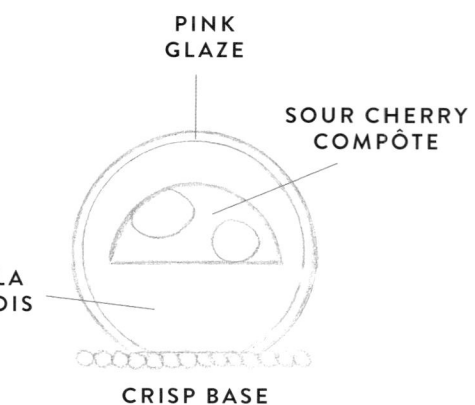

Crêpe suzette

The cold version of a delicious pancake with spicy orange coulis, fresh orange pieces, orange ice cream and slightly candied orange peel.

PANCAKE BATTER

Ingredients
300 g eggs
65 g caster sugar
500 g whole milk
½ vanilla stick
335 g flour
2 g salt
500 g whole milk
65 g butter

Preparation
Grate the vanilla and add to the milk. Beat the eggs with the caster sugar, and then add alternately the whole milk with the vanilla and the sifted flour and salt (to avoid clumping). Lastly, heat the milk and butter together (40°C), and mix in to form the batter. Pass through a fine sieve before baking.
Bake the batter in a hot pancake pan with little butter and toss the pancake after half the baking time. Spread the pancake thinly with the lightly bound orange coulis and roll it tightly. Roll up several pancakes to reach the desired diameter and cut rolls of 1 to 1.5 cm wide. Arrange different sizes of rolls on the plate.

ORANGE COULIS

Ingredients
1 clove
1 star of aniseed
½ vanilla stick
300 g fresh orange juice
110 g caster sugar
1 g agar agar
10 g Mandarine Napoléon

Preparation
In advance, infuse the herbs in the fresh orange juice (see p. 23).
Then prepare a caramel with the caster sugar and quench with the warm, infused orange juice.
Bring the resulting mixture to boil again with the agar agar and pass through a fine sieve.
Leave to cool slightly before adding the Mandarine Napoléon and place in the refrigerator.

FINISHING
Candied orange peel strips, see p. 24
Pieces of orange ('peeled alive')

ORANGE ICE CREAM

Ingredients
200 g whole milk
100 g whipped cream
100 g caster sugar
50 g glucose powder
40 g skimmed milk powder stabilizer
40 g egg yolks
425 g fresh orange juice
20 g natural concentrated orange juice (frozen)

Preparation
Mix all dry ingredients (skimmed milk powder, caster sugar, glucose powder, stabilizer). Heat the whole milk and whipped cream to 40°C and add the egg yolks and mix. Loosely beat the egg whites with a little milk or whipped cream.
Make an anglaise of the entire mixture (83°C). Pass the composition through a fine sieve and mix the ice cream for 2 minutes.
Refrigerate the ice cream mix for 12 hours. Turbine and place immediately into the selected moulds (3D quenelle).

BART'S TIPS

Make sure that the orange coulis is well bound: this brings together all the other tastes on the plate.

Brownie with chocolate mousse

A real chocolate mousse, light in texture but full of flavour!
In combination with a smooth brownie bottom and roasted hazelnut bits.

BROWNIE BATTER

Ingredients
155 g butter
80 g caster sugar
90 g dark muscovado sugar
140 g eggs
70 g flour
1 g coarse sea salt
125 g fondant chocolate

Preparation
Take the eggs out of the refrigerator and allow to reach room temperature. Soften the butter, then mix with the sugars, using the beater spatula, to give a smooth and slightly frothy mass. Then mix in the eggs one by one.
Sift and stir in the flour and coarse sea salt.
Lastly, stir in the melted chocolate (45°C) to produce a homogeneous whole.
Place the batter in a square or rectangular frame and bake at 160°C for 20 to 25 minutes (depending on the total volume).
Allow to cool completely, then cut into square or rectangular brownies.

ICING

Ingredients
550 g milk chocolate
130 g grape seed oil
120 g chopped roasted hazelnuts

Preparation
Roast the hazelnuts in advance and leave to cool. Lightly pre-crystallize the milk chocolate (30°C), and add the grape seed oil, together with the chopped roasted hazelnuts.
Dunk the pre-cut brownies (2.5 × 12 cm) into the icing and place on the plate.

CHOCOLATE MOUSSE

Ingredients
165 g sugar syrup 32°Baumé
   (75 g water and 90 g caster sugar)
100 g egg yolks
590 g cream (35%)
295 g fondant chocolate

Preparation
Prepare a pâte à bombe (French term for a dough bomb) by slowly bringing the water and the sugar to the boil. Meanwhile, beat the egg yolks with the machine till slightly frothy.
Once the sugar syrup has reached 115°C, add it to the egg yolks, pouring evenly. Leave mixer beater turning at medium speed during this process.
Then add approximately one third of the ⅔ whipped cream to the melted chocolate (45°C), if necessary, warming slightly, so that the cream and chocolate mixture maintains a temperature of 35°C.
Add to this mixture the airy, foamy dough bomb. Lastly, mix the remaining thick cream to produce a homogeneous, airy chocolate mousse.

FINISHING AND PRESENTATION

Using a toothed nozzle, pipe the chocolate mousse in a spiral shape onto the glazed brownie bottom.
Finish with a few thin lines of chocolate sprinkled with tiny crispy crispies.

Scan the QR code or go to
www.lannoopublishinggroup.com/desserts-video-en

Scan the QR code or go to
www.lannoopublishinggroup.com/desserts-video-en

BART'S TIPS

For the brownie batter, mixed all the ingredients at the same temperature. This drastically reduces the danger of curdling.

Pavlova

An historical classic bearing the name of famous Russian ballet dancer Anna Pavlova. The dessert is said to have been created in her honour. Typically it combines meringue, whipped cream, vanilla ice cream and red fruits.

VANILLA ICE CREAM

Ingredients
1 litre whole milk
400 g whipped cream (40%)
1 vanilla stick
235 g caster sugar
90 g glucose powder
70 g skimmed milk powder
stabilizer (ensures better stability and shelf life of the ice cream, amount dependent on the brand)
120 g egg yolks

Preparation
Mix the dry ingredients (caster sugar, glucose powder, skimmed milk powder, stabilizer). Heat the milk (60°C) along with the whipped cream and the cut and scraped-out vanilla stick, and then stir in the mixed dry ingredients. Beat the egg yolks loosely, mix with some lukewarm milk and add to the whole.
Continue to heat to produce an anglaise (83°C). Pass the composition immediately through a fine sieve and mix for 2 minutes (emulsifying / homogenizing). Chill the ice cream mix quickly and place it in the refrigerator (ripening process) for 12 hours.
Lastly, stir the ice cream mix into a spoonable mass and use or store at once.
Place the resulting vanilla ice cream into 5 cm diameter hemispheres and freeze. Then dip the ice in dip chocolate.

WHITE CHOCOLATE DIP

Ingredients
450 g white chocolate
75 g cocoa butter
60 g almond bars, roasted and chopped

Preparation
Chop and roast the almond bars in advance and leave to cool. Melt the cocoa butter and white chocolate together (40°C) and add the chopped almond bars.
Immerse the frozen vanilla ice cream (-20°C) into the chocolate dip (32°C) and store or serve.

FRENCH MERINGUE

Ingredients
200 g egg white
200 g caster sugar
180 g icing sugar

Preparation
Beat the egg-white and gradually add the caster sugar. Beat to a firm but smooth foam.
Lastly, fold in the sifted icing sugar. Using a smooth nozzle, pipe in fine lines onto silicone baking mats and bake at 100°C for about two hours.
Leave the meringues to cool completely before breaking into the desired pieces, and then keep dry in a sealed container.

WHIPPED CREAM

Ingredients
500 g whipped cream
45 g caster sugar

Preparation
Beat the cream with the caster sugar at medium speed into a firm but smooth, pipeable cream. Using a toothed nozzle, place a spiral of whipped cream onto the vanilla ice cream.

/// CONSTRUCTION ///

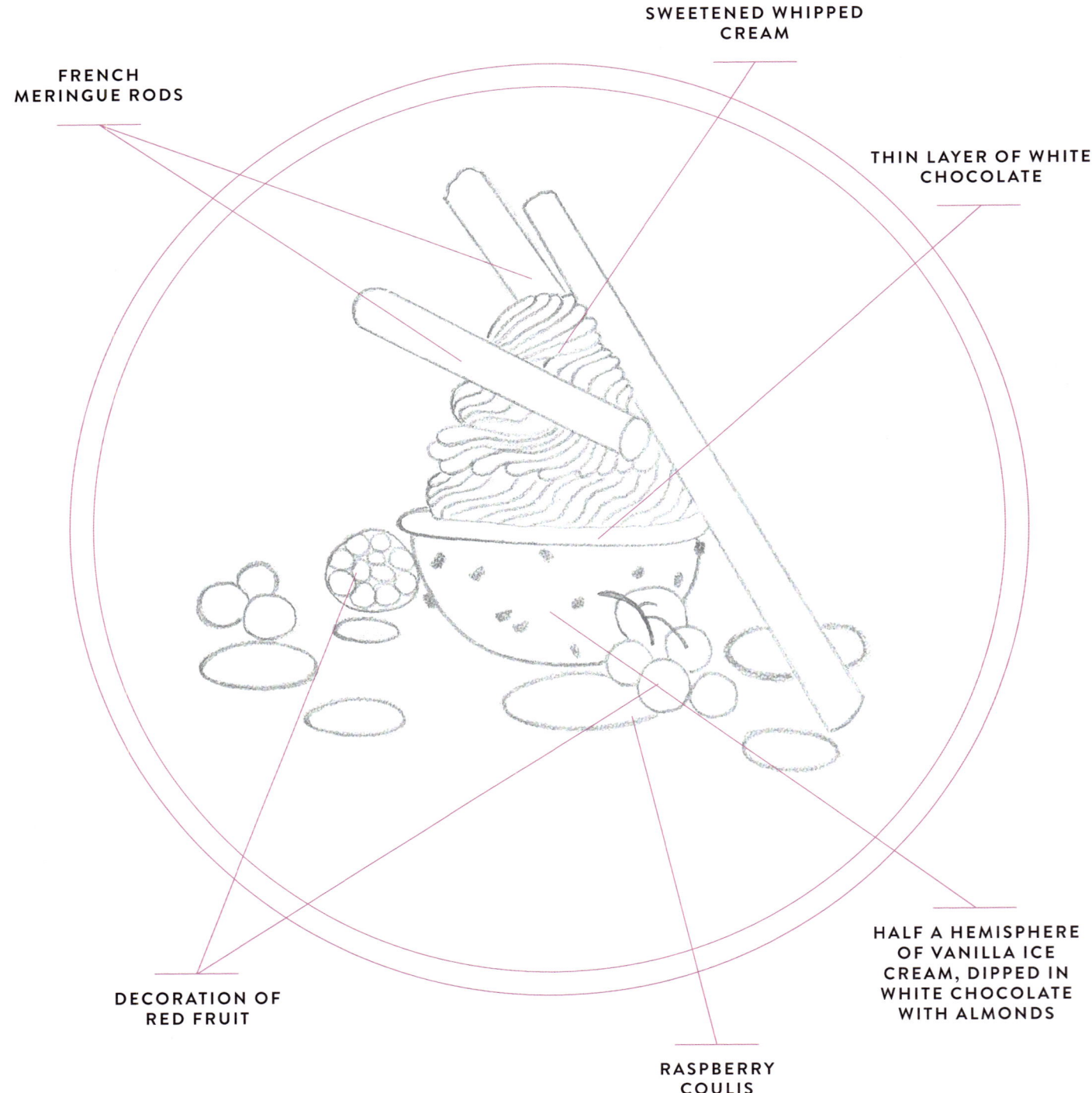

- FRENCH MERINGUE RODS
- SWEETENED WHIPPED CREAM
- THIN LAYER OF WHITE CHOCOLATE
- HALF A HEMISPHERE OF VANILLA ICE CREAM, DIPPED IN WHITE CHOCOLATE WITH ALMONDS
- RASPBERRY COULIS
- DECORATION OF RED FRUIT

RASPBERRY COULIS

Ingredients
250 g raspberry purée with
    10% sugar
30 g caster sugar

Preparation
Dissolve the sugar in the purée.

COMPOSING THE DESSERT
Dip the hemispherical ball of vanilla ice cream coated with white chocolate onto the plate, cover with a thin layer of white chocolate of slightly larger diameter (see decoration techniques on p. 31). Add a spiral of whipped cream and garnish with the thin sticks of crispy meringue.
Finish with the raspberry coulis and red fruit.

Lemon pie

Fresh-sour classic with the powerful combination of lemon-lime crémeux, crispy biscuit, soft meringue and red fruit.

BUTTER DOUGH

Ingredients
250 g butter
165 g icing sugar
65 g almond powder 100%
2 g vanilla powder (100% vanilla stick)
95 g egg yolks
470 g flour
3 g coarse sea salt

Preparation
Before starting, leave the butter to reach room temperature. Then mix the butter with the icing sugar, almond powder and vanilla powder. Mix the egg yolks well and add. When well mixed, fold in the sifted flour and salt to produce a homogeneous dough.
Chill the dough (3°C) before processing further.
Roll the chilled butter dough out to 2.5 mm thick and cut 12mm wide strips. Place these in metal rings of the desired size and bake at 160°C.
Bake for about 18 minutes until golden brown.

LEMON CREAM

Ingredients
125 g fresh lemon juice
125 g fresh lime juice
grated zest of 1 lime
150 g caster sugar
160 g eggs
140 g egg yolks
30 g gelatine (or 2½ gelatine leaves)
150 g butter

Preparation
Pre-soak the gelatine. Make an anglaise (83°C) with the first six ingredients and then add the soaked gelatine. Allow to cool to 38°C before adding the soft butter to give a smooth emulsion/ crémeux. Place the crémeux into a 3D silicone ball mat, and freeze for further use.
Glaze the resulting lemon-lime crémeux with a neutral jelly to which a little lime juice (or else lime zest) and a few drops of yellow liquid colouring are added. Heat the glacé icing to 50°C to obtain optimal and thin adhesion around the crémeux.

ITALIAN FOAM

Ingredients
80 g water
300 g caster sugar
200 g egg white
30 g caster sugar

Preparation
Bring the water and most of the caster sugar to the boil.
Once the sugar syrup has boiled, beat the egg whites and the caster sugar together at medium speed.
Boil the sugar water up to 121°C, then add it in a smooth jet to the already firm, but smoothly beaten egg-whites.
Beat this 'Italian foam' at medium speed until cold.

DECORATION
Thin (1 mm) layer of coloured chocolate – see chocolate techniques on p. 31
Small pieces of ground Napoleon candy (sweet-sour hard-boiled sweets), see p. 163

/// CONSTRUCTION ///

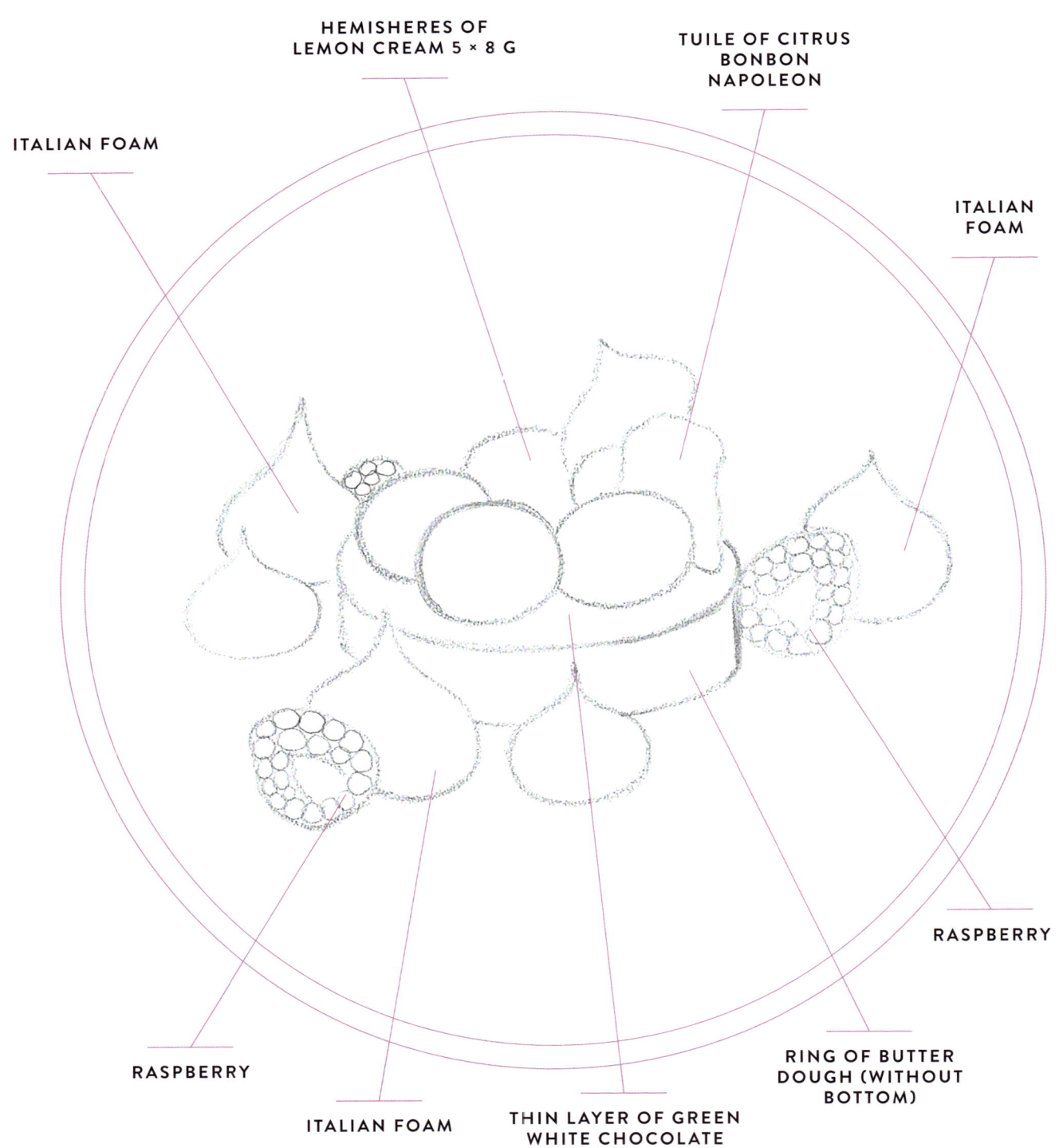

- HEMISHERES OF LEMON CREAM 5 × 8 G
- TUILE OF CITRUS BONBON NAPOLEON
- ITALIAN FOAM
- ITALIAN FOAM
- RASPBERRY
- RING OF BUTTER DOUGH (WITHOUT BOTTOM)
- THIN LAYER OF GREEN WHITE CHOCOLATE
- ITALIAN FOAM
- RASPBERRY

BART'S TIPS

Do not bake the butter dough at a high temperature, but let it bake / dry (at 160 °C) for maximum moisture removal and optimum crispness of the final result.

Fill the tart ring only at the edges. The centre can eventually be filled afterwards with a layer of crumble or ground butter dough.

Essential classics

Dame blanche

*Another major classic: vanilla ice cream with whipped cream,
a biscuit as a crunch and a delicious hot chocolate sauce poured over it. An absolute topper!*

VANILLA ICE CREAM

Ingredients
1 litre whole milk
400 g whipped cream (40%)
1 vanilla stick
235 g caster sugar
90 g glucose powder
70 g skimmed milk powder
stabilizer (ensures better stability
   and shelf life of the ice cream,
   amount dependent on the brand)
120 g egg yolks

Preparation
Mix the dry ingredients (caster sugar, glucose powder, skimmed milk powder, stabilizer). Heat the milk (60°C) along with the whipped cream and the cut and scraped-out vanilla stick, and then stir in the mixed dry ingredients. Beat the egg yolks loosely, mix with some lukewarm milk and add to the whole.
Continue to heat to produce an anglaise (83°C). Pass the composition immediately through a fine sieve and mix for 2 minutes (emulsifying / homogenizing). Let the ice cream mix chill quickly and place it in the refrigerator (ripening process) for 12 hours.
Lastly, stir the ice cream mix into a spoonable mass and store or use at once. For the ice cream in the photo we have used 3D 30 gram silicone moulds.

CHOCOLATE SAUCE

Ingredients
250 g whole milk
250 g cream (35%)
300 g fondant chocolate

Preparation
Heat the milk and cream together to 60°C and gradually add to the fondant chocolate. Mix steadily until the chocolate is completely absorbed into the mass.
Finally, mix the mass into an emulsion (homogeneous mass).
Keep cool at 3°C and heat the required amount of chocolate sauce just before serving.

/// CONSTRUCTION ///

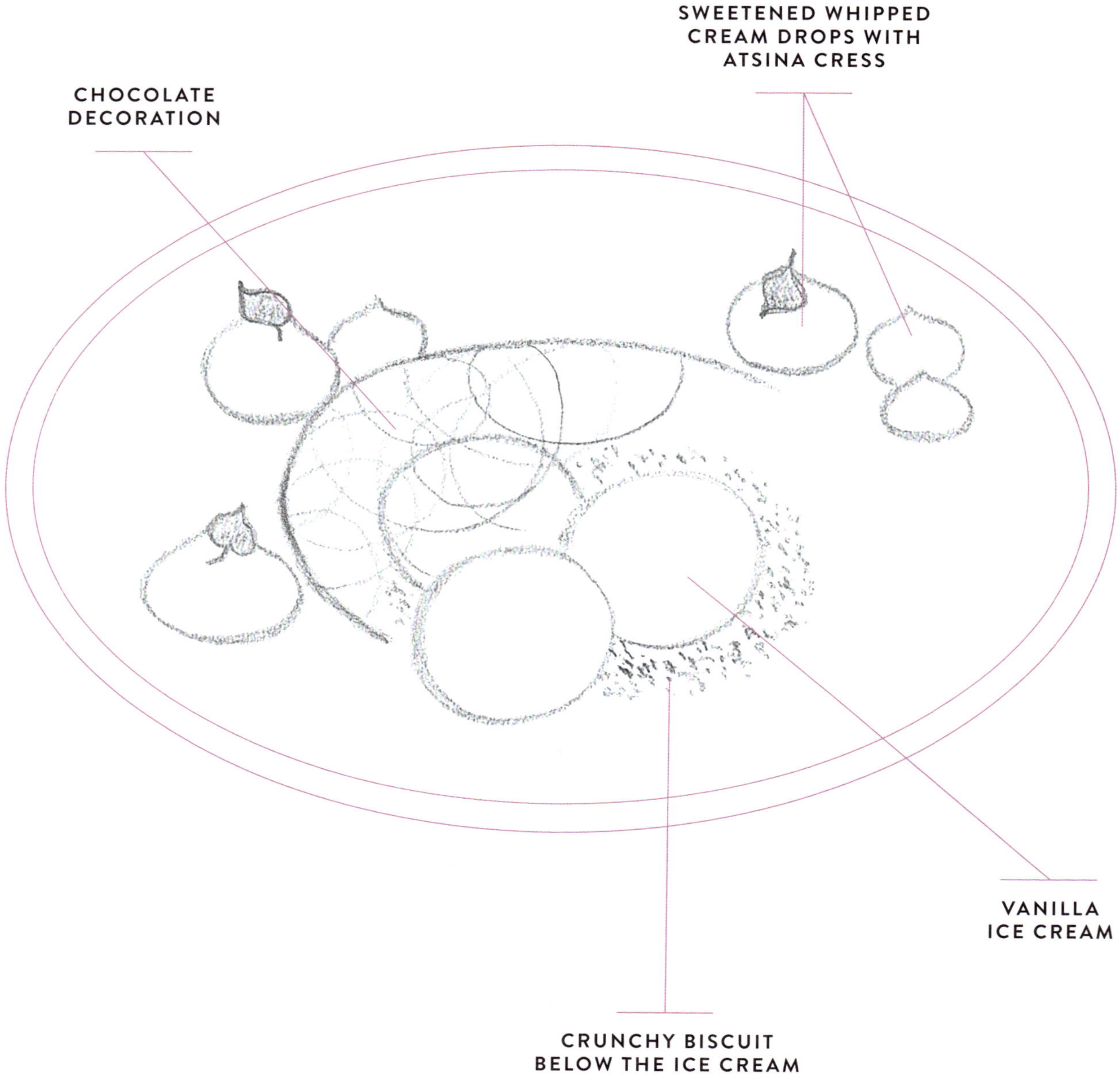

CHOCOLATE DECORATION

SWEETENED WHIPPED CREAM DROPS WITH ATSINA CRESS

VANILLA ICE CREAM

CRUNCHY BISCUIT BELOW THE ICE CREAM

CRUNCHY BISCUIT (TARTINE RUSSE)

Ingredients
130 g butter
45 g cassonade (soft brown sugar)
90 g caster sugar
145 g flour
1 g vanilla powder (100% vanilla stick)
1 g coarse sea salt

Preparation
Cream the butter into a soft, smooth crème and add both sugars. Fold in the mixed and sifted flour, cocoa powder and coarse sea salt to produce a homogenous mass.
Roll out the dough evenly on a silicone mat and bake at 220°C for seven minutes.
Leave to cool completely and break or mix the baked crispy biscuit to produce the desired crunch.

WHIPPED CREAM DROPS

Ingredients
500 g whipped cream
45 g caster sugar

Preparation
Beat the cream with the caster sugar at medium speed into a firm but smooth, pipeable cream. Apply attractive drops to the edge of the plate with a smooth nozzle.

FINISHING
Atsina cress (on the whipped cream)
Chocolate decoration on p. 29

Île flottante (floating island)

Foamy, airy little islands floating in a fresh vanilla sauce with an accent of red fruit.

CRÈME ANGLAISE

Ingredients
350 g whole milk
150 g cream (35%)
¾ vanilla stick
120 g egg yolks
65 g sugar

Preparation
Prepare an anglaise. For this, heat the whole milk with the cream and the scraped-out vanilla stick to 50°C and add part of this mixture to the loosely beaten egg yolks and the sugar. Add the rest and heat to 83°C, stirring all the time. Once the desired temperature is mixed, pour the mixture through a fine sieve and cover with cling film. Chill to 3°C.

COLD FOAM (MERINGUE)

Ingredients
200 g egg white
200 g caster sugar

Preparation
Beat the egg white in a clean, fat-free bowl together with the caster sugar (add gradually), to produce a firm but smooth foam.
Pipe little balls of foam (islands) with a plain nozzle onto a piece of baking paper and cook for 10 to 15 seconds in a microwave at medium power.
The resulting foam balls are now much easier to manipulate and move about. Afterwards, they can be sprinkled with powdered sugar on top and then caramelized briefly with a branding iron or gas burner.

THIN, TRANSPARENT ISOMALT DECORATION

Sprinkle a small amount of isomalt sugar onto an upturned baking plate with a silicone baking mat. Cover with a second silicone mat, together with a baking plate (weight) and allow the sugar to melt completely in the oven at 150°C. Leave to cool completely before removing the baking mats.
After that, break the sugar to the desired size.

COMPOSITION AND PRESENTATION

Place the cold anglaise (3°C) in a plate or bowl of your choice.
Let the garnished meringues float on the cold anglaise and finish with pieces of red fruit, an accent of lime zest and eventually small broken pieces of isomalt decoration.

BART'S TIPS

Serve with a pre-made and well-chilled crème anglaise. In this way the overall dessert will taste a lot fresher.

Tiramisu

This Italian dessert is characterized by the airy, creamy crème of mascarpone in combination with biscuit (or cake) saturated with a mixture of cold coffee and coffee liqueur and finished with cocoa powder. A dash of chocolate sabayon and a crispy biscuit give this dessert a certain added value.

TIRAMISU CRÈME

Ingredients
25 g water
75 g caster sugar
100 g egg white
10 g caster sugar
500 g mascarpone
60 g pasteurized egg yolks

Preparation
Boil the water with the sugar to 110°C, then slowly start to beat the egg whites with the small amount of caster sugar. Only when the sugar syrup has reached 121°C can it be added to the firm but smoothly whipped egg whites (boiled foam). Leave to cool, but keep it moving in the mixer to maintain an even consistency.
Mix the mascarpone and the loosely beaten pasteurized yolks. Then mix in the almost cold boiled foam.
Place the Tiramisu crème into a silicone mould of your choice (see photo) and finish with a thick layer of very well-imbibed biscuit. Freeze before taking out of the mould for further finishing.

AIRY SOFT BISCUIT (ABLE TO ABSORB LOTS OF COFFEE SYRUP – DUCHESSE BISCUIT)

Ingredients
225 g eggs
110 g caster sugar
110 g flour
65 g ground almonds 1/1
25 g butter

Preparation
Beat the butter and sugar together with a beater into an airy mass. Heat slightly to obtain an airy and sufficiently stiff mass. Then, with a spatula, lightly fold in the sifted mixture of flour and ground almonds. Lastly mix in the melted butter (40°C) and spread out evenly on a 40 × 30 cm baking tray.
Bake at 220°C for around ten minutes. Cut to the desired size and soak both sides well with the coffee syrup.

TIRAMISU COFFEE SAUCE SYRUP

Ingredients
250 ml pure coffee
85 g amaretto (sweet almond liqueur with Italian roots)

Preparation
Mix the amaretto with the cold coffee.

/// CONSTRUCTION ///

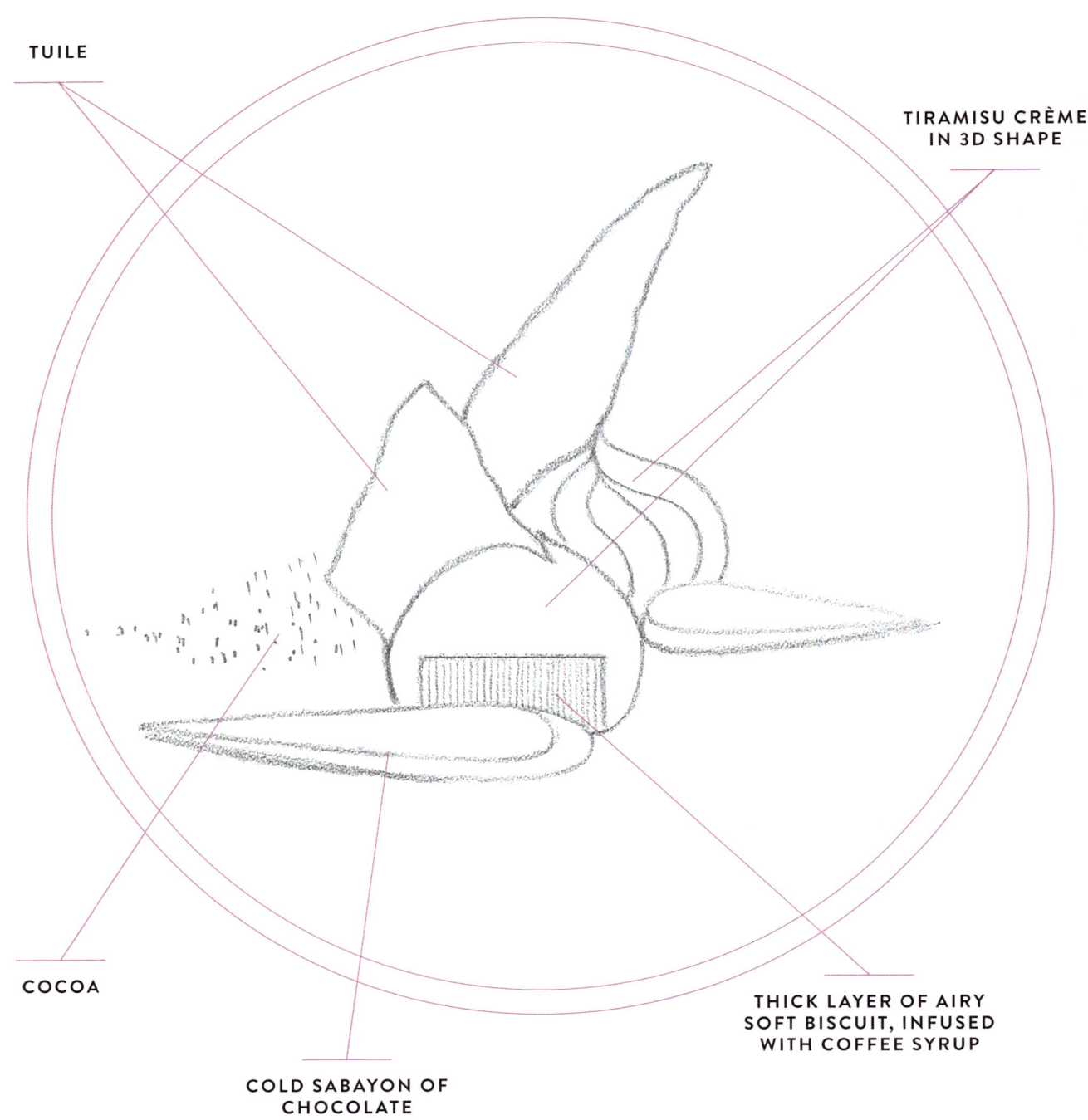

TUILE

TIRAMISU CRÈME IN 3D SHAPE

COCOA

COLD SABAYON OF CHOCOLATE

THICK LAYER OF AIRY SOFT BISCUIT, INFUSED WITH COFFEE SYRUP

COLD SABAYON OF CHOCOLATE AND ITALIAN DESSERT WINE

Ingredients
150 g marsala (Sicilian fortified dessert wine)
150 g egg yolks
100 g caster sugar
10 g cocoa powder
300 g cream (35%)

Preparation
Make a sabayon of the marsala, egg yolks, caster sugar and cocoa powder. Heat, stirring all the time to à la nappe consistency (83°C). Allow the sabayon to cool completely (3°C) and lastly fold in the 2/3 whipped cream.
Use this as a soft supplementary cream to combine with the tiramisu.

TUILE (CRISPY BISCUIT)

Ingredients
125 g butter
2 g vanilla essence
125 g egg white (at room temperature)
125 g icing sugar
150 g flour
2 g salt

Preparation
Cream the butter and vanilla into a soft, smooth crème and mix in the icing sugar. Blend in the egg whites, yolks, followed by the sifted mixture of flour and salt.
Roll out the dough onto a Silpat mat with a pre-cut template (rectangle) and bake until golden brown at 200°C. Leave to cool completely and break into pieces.

FINISHING
Take the chilled tiramisu out of the moulds and cover partially with piping chocolate (mix of 50% milk chocolate and 50% cocoa butter). Sprinkle lightly with cocoa powder.
Finish with a crème of the cold sabayon cream and some broken pieces of the crispy biscuit.

BART'S TIPS

Be sure to have a good ratio of fresh mascarpone to tiramisu crème and a flat biscuit duchesse well-soaked with the coffee-liqueur syrup.

Tarte tatin

Crunchy puff pastry base, with cooked apples in the caramel and a quenelle of vanilla ice cream.

PREPARATION AND REROLLING (TOURER) OF THE PUFF PASTRY INVERSÉ (REVERSE PROCESSING)

See p. 25.

PROCESSING/ROLLING OF PUFF PASTRY

Roll out the desired amount of touré puff pastry to 3 mm thick and place on a lined baking tray. Cover the rolled-out dough with cling film and leave for a few hours at 3°C. Leaving freshly rolled puff pastry to rest is important to prevent the dough shrinking during baking.

Place the puff pastry in the oven and bake at 180°C for 30-40 minutes until golden brown.

Tip: Place a sheet of baking paper and a grid or light plate on top of the puff pastry to ensure even working and volume of the puff pastry. Remove immediately after baking.

TO CARAMELIZE PUFF PASTRY

Using a fine sieve, sprinkle a uniform layer of icing sugar on the cooled, golden brown baked pastry, and bake for a further 4 to 5 minutes at 230°C. The layer of icing sugar will caramelize and add value to the puff pastry.

Cut the desired shapes from the caramelized puff pastry and keep dry.

CARAMELIZED APPLES

Ingredients
4 Jonagold apples
40 g butter
½ vanilla stick
a little grated lime zest
180 g caster sugar

Preparation
Dice the Jonagold apples into uniform cubes of about 5mm on each side and cook lightly with the butter on a low flame. Drain a little and then add the scraped-out vanilla stick with a little lime rasp.

Add the preparation, still hot, step by step to a just-made caramel (caster sugar) and mix well together.

Leave to cool completely at 3°C.

Stir the brunoise of caramelized apples gently and place in a sieve. The small amount of apple-caramel juice released can be used as coulis.

Presentation
Cover the bottom of a mould with a slice of caramelized puff pastry, and press the slightly heated and drained caramelized brunoise in on top. Remove the mould.

LIME AND ORANGE CRUMBLE

Ingredients
150 g butter
150 g caster sugar
grated zest of 1 lime
grated zest of 1 orange
135 g almond powder
140 g flour
2 g salt

Preparation
Mix the butter (at room temperature) with the caster sugar, grated citrus zest and almond powder. Fold in the sieved flour with the salt to produce an even dough.
Crumble the butter dough onto a baking plate and bake at 150°C. During the baking process mix the crumble to produce an optimum and evenly baked golden-brown colour.
Leave to cool completely before cutting/mixing the crumble to the desired size.

VANILLA ICE CREAM

Ingredients
1 litre whole milk
400 g whipped cream (40%)
1 vanilla stick
235 g caster sugar
90 g glucose powder
70 g skimmed milk powder
stabilizer (ensures better stability and shelf life of the ice cream, amount dependent on the brand)
120 g egg yolks

Preparation
Mix the dry ingredients (caster sugar, glucose powder, skimmed milk powder, stabilizer). Heat the milk (60°C) with the scraped-out vanilla stick, and then stir in the mixed dry ingredients. Beat the egg yolks loosely, mix with some lukewarm milk and add to the whole. Heat and stir further to produce an anglaise (83 °C), pass the composition immediately through a fine sieve and mix for 2 minutes (to emulsify/homogenize).
Let the ice cream mix cool quickly and place in the refrigerator (ripening) for 12 hours.
Lastly, churn the ice cream mix to a spoonable whole and use or store at once.

Further explanation on the different steps of ice cream preparation can be found on p. 18.

FINISHING
Finish with the apple-caramel sauce and a sprig of apple blossom on the vanilla ice.

BART'S TIPS

Not only the correct 'touring', but also the intermediate cooling (in the refrigerator) and respecting the rest periods of the dough are important for good puffing during baking (see also p. 25).

Leave the dough to cool completely before caramelizing at a high temperature in the oven. In this way the colour of the puff pastry remains stable and only the top layer caramelizes. Combine a decoration of Granny Smith apples with the tarte tatin, not only for the decorative aspect, but also for the crunchy texture that fits perfectly with the caramelized Jonagold.

Make sure you have golden brown well-baked caramelized puff pastry to guarantee optimum crispness with the lukewarm caramelized apples.

CHAPTER 3

DESSERTS WITH FRUIT AND CHOCOLATE

Raspberry – strawberry almond milk – lemongrass

A fresh little dessert with a variety of raspberries and strawberry textures, with almond milk ice and a lemongrass espuma added as a fresh-sour pendant.

ALMOND MILK ICE

Ingredients
750 g whole milk
295 g cream (40%)
320 g almond milk
50 g skimmed milk powder
60 g caster sugar
30 g glucose powder stabilizer

Preparation
Mix all the dry ingredients (skimmed milk powder, caster sugar, glucose powder and stabilizer).
Heat the milk, cream and almond milk to 40°C and fold in the dry ingredients.
Heat, stirring all the time to 83°C to produce an anglaise, pass through a fine sieve and mix in the almond milk ice (homogenizing).
Leave the ice to cool for 12 hours at 3°C (ripening process).
Churn the almond milk ice and immediately fill the 3D quenelle moulds. Freeze.

RASPBERRY CRUNCH

Add raspberry powder to pre-crystallized white chocolate and mix with rice pops. Spread on baking paper, and when fully crystallized, break by hand or with a cutter to the desired size.

LIGHTLY BOUND RASPBERRY COULIS

Ingredients
500 g raspberry purée with 10% sugar
40 g caster sugar
66 g gelatine (or 5½ gelatine leaves)
15 g raspberry liqueur

Preparation
Heat the raspberry purée with the sugar to 45°C and add the soaked gelatine. Wait until the gelatine is completely absorbed and add the raspberry liqueur. Pour the raspberry coulis into a Silpat silicone backing mat (3 mm deep) and freeze for further use.
Once cool and sufficiently stiff, cut out circles of various small diameters.

RED FRUIT GEL

Ingredients
85 g strawberries
85 g raspberry purée with 10% sugar
85 g cherry purée with 10% sugar
50 g sugar water 1/1
2 g agar agar

Preparation
Mix the fresh strawberries with the fruit purées, pass through a fine sieve and bring slowly to the boil with the sugar water and the agar agar.
Pour immediately through a fine sieve and store at 3°C.
Mix to a smooth gel just before use.

/// CONSTRUCTION ///

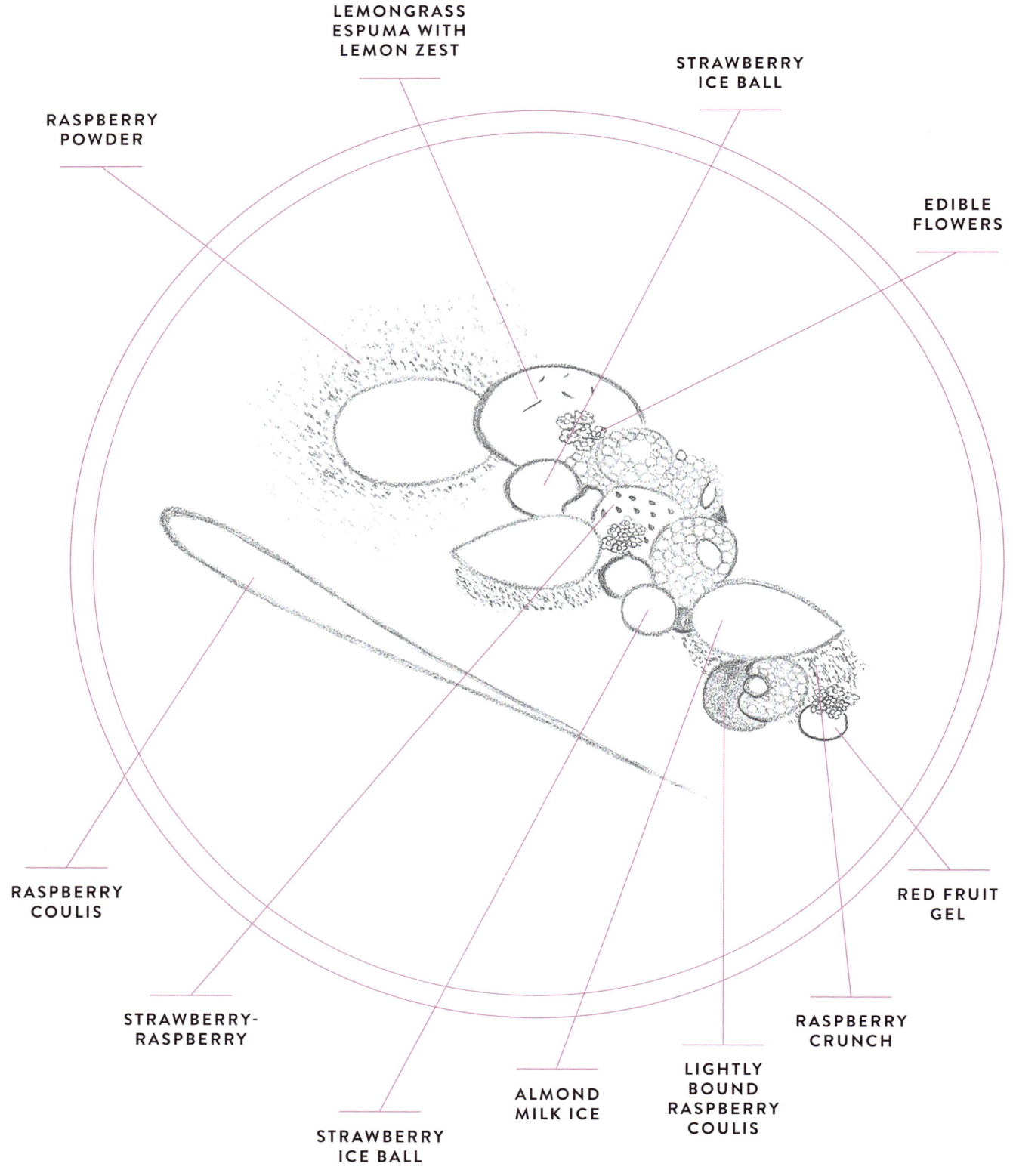

LEMONGRASS ESPUMA

Ingredients
100 g whole milk
125 g cream (35%)
25 g lime juice
zest of 1 lime
2 stalks of lemongrass
40 g egg yolks
25 g caster sugar

Preparation
Cut the lemongrass stalks into pieces (cover with cling film). Then bring the milk with the cream, the lime juice and the zest to the boil, add the lemongrass and leave to infuse until cool.
Push the infused mixture through a fine sieve, add the yolks and caster sugar to heat and stir to 83°C to produce an anglaise. Pour through a fine sieve again and leave to cool at 3°C for some hours. Then place the cold mass into a siphon bottle with a gas cartridge (N2O), then mix by shaking the siphon bottle well (good distribution of the gas). If necessary, use a second gas cartridge to obtain an attractive, airy and shiny espuma.

STRAWBERRY ICE BALL

Ingredients
200 g purée of fresh strawberries
10 g lime juice
165 g sugar syrup (65 g water and 35 g caster sugar)
1 g xanthan gum (cold binder)

Preparation
Mix the strawberries with the lime juice, sugar syrup and cold binder.
Place 1 cm diameter balls in a 3D silicone mat and freeze before use. Add immediately before serving.

FINISHING
Fresh strawberries
Fresh raspberries
Crossed raspberry-strawberry
Edible flowers
Lime zest
Raspberry powder

BART'S TIPS

Strawberry ice balls (maximum 1 cm diameter) can be a nice alternative to dripping coulis in liquid nitrogen.

Chocolate – Rodenbach – red fruits

In this dessert, the taste of a Flemish red-brown beer with an almost 200 year-old history is beautifully harmonized with chocolate and red fruit flavours. The addition of a cream caramel (dulce de leche) and a crispy crumble at the bottom of dessert add further value.

ROLL OF FRUITY GANACHE

Ingredients
300 g whipped cream (40%)
150 g raspberry purée
50 g glucose
45 g caster sugar
1 g salt
3 g agar agar
120 g Jivara milk chocolate
70 g fondant chocolate
36 g gelatine (or 3 gelatine leaves)

Preparation
Bring the first six ingredients to the boil and add gradually to both chocolates until these are completely absorbed in the mass. Last of all add the soaked gelatine and mix everything to a smooth emulsion.
Place the emulsion in the desired silicone baking mat (mini interior) or pour into a silicone baking tray and cut to size and shape afterwards.
Cool for use.

SOUR CHERRY (GRIOTTE) CRÉMEUX

Ingredients
300 g griotte purée
120 g egg yolks
90 g eggs
70 g caster sugar
36 g gelatine (or 3 gelatine leaves)
110 g butter

Preparation
Heat and stir the first four ingredients to produce an anglaise (83°C), remove from the heat and add the soaked gelatine. Pass through a fine sieve and mix in the soft butter at 38°C to give a smooth cream (crémeux).
Place the crémeux in a 3D balls mat and cool well in the freezer.
Remove the sour cherry crémeux balls from the mould and glaze with a dark red glaze. For this, mix a neutral jelly with 15-20% (sour) cherry purée, a little red liquid colouring and heat to 50°C for glazing.

CRÈME OF CREAM CARAMEL (DULCE DE LECHE)

Ingredients
200 g cream (35%)
1 vanilla stick
160 g egg yolks
55 g caster sugar
55 g cream caramel powder
54 g gelatine (of 4 ½ gelatine leaves)
200 g cream (35%)

Preparation
Heat and stir the ingredients to form an anglaise (83°C). Remove from the heat and add the soaked gelatine. Pass through a fine sieve. Leave the mixture to cool to 25-30°C, then fold in the ⅔ whipped cream. Stir to a smooth crème.
Place the cream caramel crème in a 3D ball mat of the desired diameter and cool sufficiently before removing.
Sprinkle the crème with a little cream caramel powder before serving.

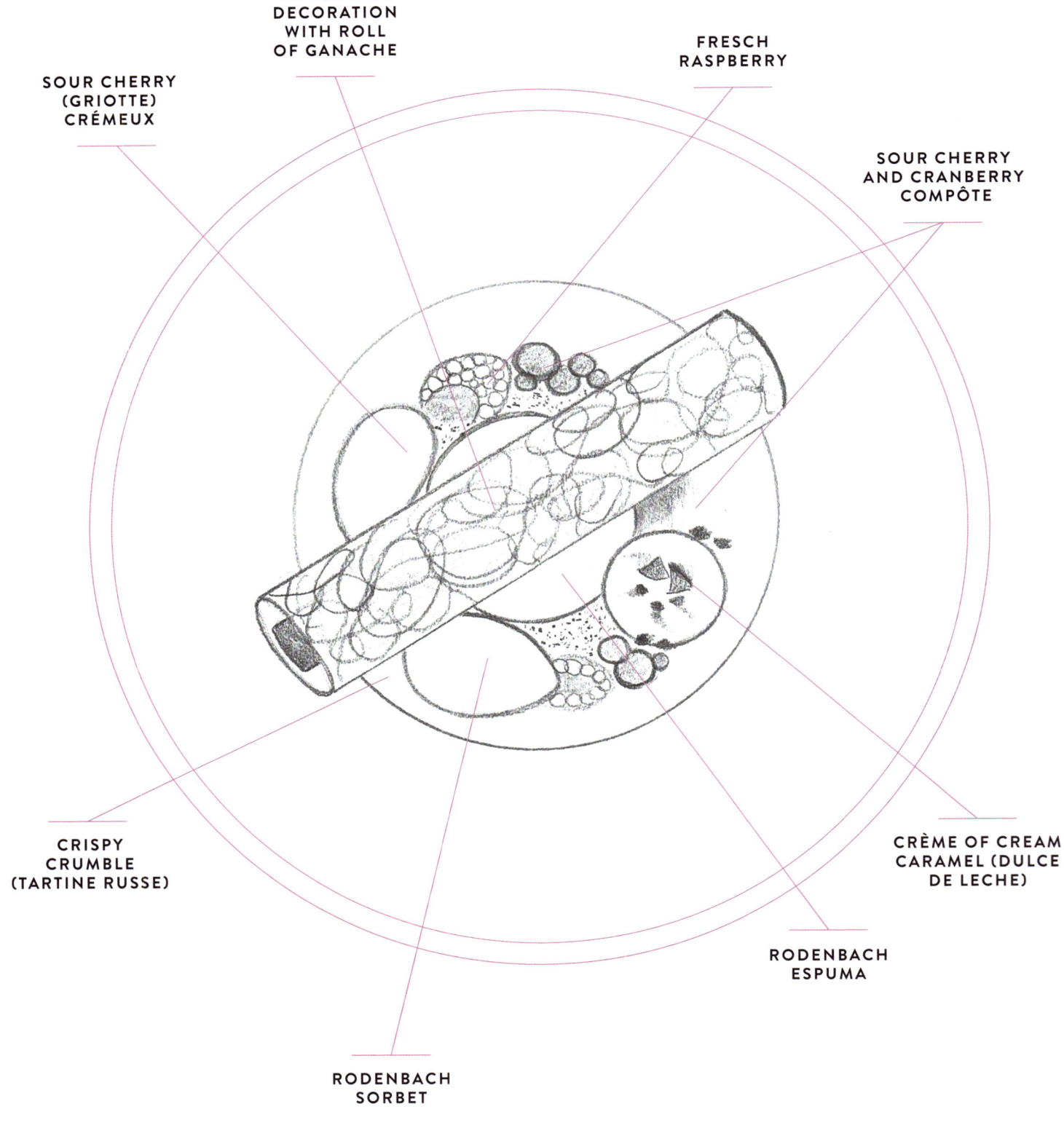

RODENBACH ESPUMA

Ingredients
105 g cream (35%)
50 g caster sugar
18 g gelatine (or 1½ gelatine leaves)
250 g Rodenbach, fruity character with an alcohol volume of 5.2%

Preparation
Heat the cream with the sugar to around 40°C and add the soaked gelatine. Then mix in the Rodenbach. Mix and sieve the espuma.

Place this espuma into a siphon with a single gas cartridge (N2O) and cool for a few hours in the refrigerator (3°C). If necessary, add another gas cartridge until the espuma has the desired firmness. Always shake the siphon bottle well to ensure optimal gas distribution.

RODENBACH SORBET

Ingredients
200 g sugar syrup (32° Baumé; see also p. 24)
75 g caster sugar
30 g glucose powder
25 g whole milk powder
combined sorbet stabilizer (emulsifier and stabilizer)
750 ml Rodenbach
a few drops of red wine vinegar (sauvignon vinegar)

Preparation
Heat the sugar syrup to 50°C and mix with the mixed dry ingredients (caster sugar, glucose powder, milk powder and combined sorbet stabilizer). Leave this syrup to cool for a few hours at 3°C (refrigerator) and add the cold beer and possibly the red wine vinegar just before churning.

Churn the sorbet in the ice cream maker and immediately fill the 3D quenelle moulds. Freeze this sufficiently before removing from the moulds for further use.

CRISPY CRUMBLE (TARTINE RUSSE)

Ingredients
165 g butter
110 g caster sugar
55 g soft brown sugar
180 g flour
1.5 g coarse sea salt

Preparation
Cream the butter and fold in both sugars. Add the mixed flour and sea salt and mix well.

Spread the mixture evenly onto a Silpat baking mat and bake golden brown at 210°C. Allow to cool completely and crunch to the desired size.

SOUR CHERRY AND CRANBERRY COMPÔTE

Ingredients
220 g sour cherry purée with 10% sugar
70 g raspberry purée with 10% sugar
170 g cranberries
100 g caster sugar
8 g pectin

Preparation
Heat the fruit together with three-quarters of the caster sugar. Just before boiling point add the remaining caster sugar mixed with the pectin. Bring gently to the boil for a few minutes.

Pour into a plastic container, cover with cling film and allow to cool completely (3°C).

FINISHING
Fresh raspberries
Spiral (tube) made from milk chocolate (see chocolate techniques on p. 31).
Cream caramel powder (dulce de leche)

BART'S TIPS

Place the roll of fruity ganache in the chocolate decoration, both as an eye-catcher and to provide textural variation.

Yoghurt – passionfruit – mango lime – white chocolate

A dessert with yoghurt in the main role. Passion fruit, mango and an accent of coconut provide an exotic touch. The soft crème structures alternate with the crispy-crunchy bottom to give greater depth to the dessert.

EXOTIC CRISPY-CRUNCHY BOTTOM

Ingredients
20 g Wet Proof crispy passion fruit, lightly chopped if necessary (Sosa)
15 g popping sugar drops
20 g ground coconut, lightly roasted
25 g feuilletine
65 g crumble or ground cookies
5 g yoghurt powder
80 g white chocolate
10 g grape seed oil

Preparation
Stir the dry ingredients together (first six ingredients) and mix with the mixture of molten white chocolate and oil. Spread out immediately 3 mm thick in a ring mould or Silpat baking mat (doughnut shape), press well and cool for further preparation.

---

* *Mix 50% white chocolate with 50% cocoa butter and atomize with a high pressure spray gun onto the cold crème.*

PASSIONFRUIT CRÉMEUX

Ingredients
250 g passionfruit juice with 10% sugar
120 g egg yolks
70 g caster sugar
24 g gelatine (or 2 gelatine leaves)
85 g butter (pre-softened)

Preparation
Heat and stir the first three ingredients to produce an anglaise (83°C). Remove from the heat and add the soaked gelatine. Pour through a fine sieve and mix in the butter at 38°C to produce an emulsion (homogeneous mass).
Place the passionfruit crémeux into a 3D quenelle baking mat and cool before proceeding further.
Glaze the resulting quenelle with a neutral jelly to which 15-20% passionfruit purée and a few drops of yellow liquid colouring have been added. Use the glacé icing at 50°C to ensure a thin, tight layer around the quenelle.

CRÈME OF YOGHURT AND LIME

Ingredients
240 g whole milk
60 g lime juice
1 vanilla stick
240 g caster sugar
108 g gelatine (or 9 gelatine leaves)
150 g Greek yoghurt
30 g yoghurt powder
630 g cream (35%)

Preparation
Bring the milk gently to the boil with the lime juice, the scraped vanilla stick and the caster sugar. Remove from the heat. After a few minutes, pour the mixture through a fine sieve onto the soaked gelatine.
Mix the Greek yoghurt and the yoghurt powder together and then fold into the other ingredients.
At a temperature of 25°C, mix the 2/3 whipped cream lightly into the whole to produce a smooth crème.
Using a smooth nozzle, pipe uneven drops onto baking paper and spray with white chocolate spray mix* for a velvety effect (after cooling).

/// CONSTRUCTION ///

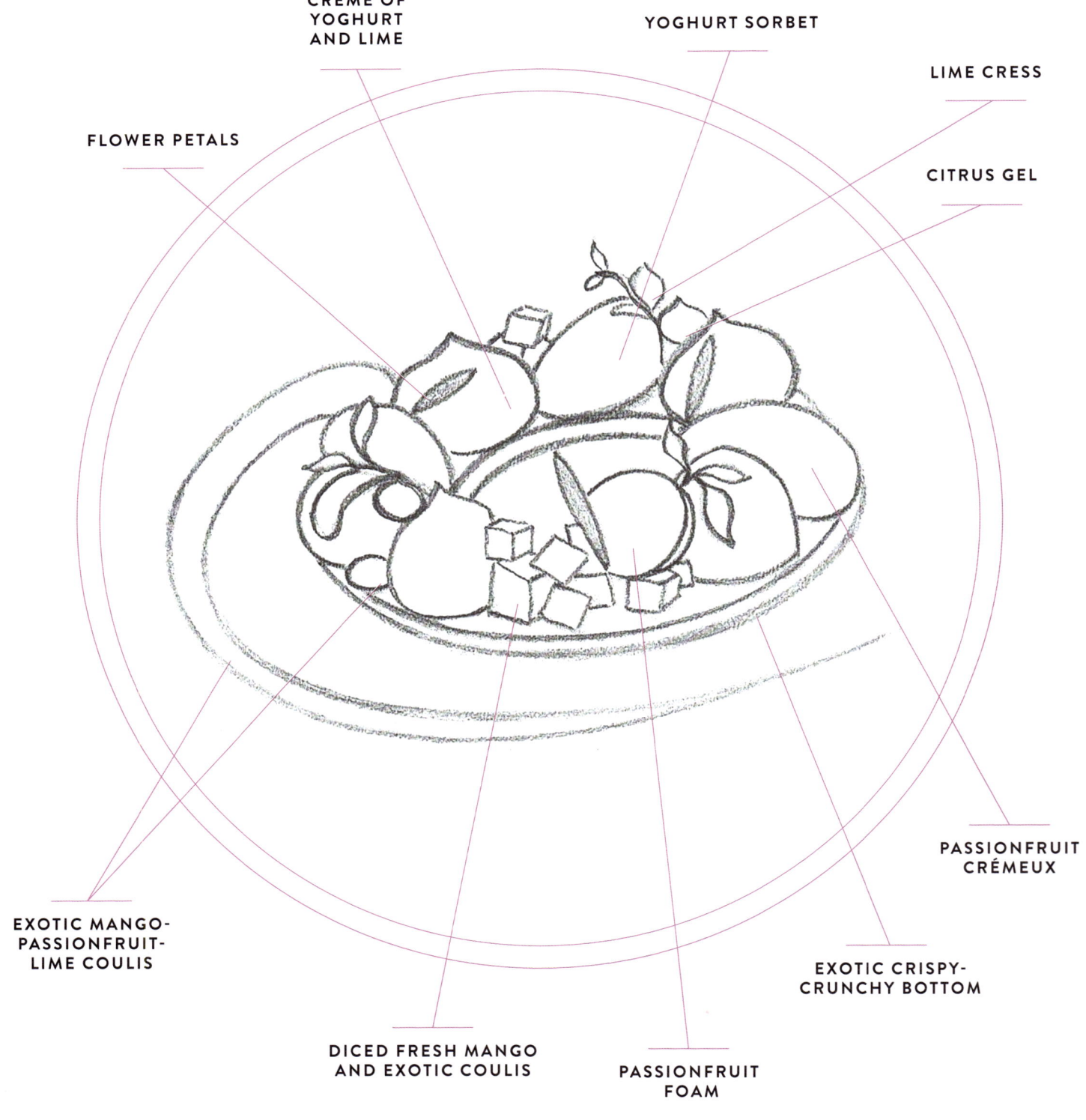

- CRÈME OF YOGHURT AND LIME
- YOGHURT SORBET
- LIME CRESS
- CITRUS GEL
- FLOWER PETALS
- PASSIONFRUIT CRÉMEUX
- EXOTIC CRISPY-CRUNCHY BOTTOM
- PASSIONFRUIT FOAM
- DICED FRESH MANGO AND EXOTIC COULIS
- EXOTIC MANGO-PASSIONFRUIT-LIME COULIS

YOGHURT SORBET

Ingredients
65 g water
135 g caster sugar
55 g glucose powder
25 g dextrose
combined sorbet stabilizer (emulsifier and stabilizer)
665 g Greek yoghurt, natural
Zest of ⅓ lime

Preparation
Mix the dry ingredients (caster sugar, glucose powder, dextrose and combined stabilizer) and heat in the water until all the sugars are dissolved (50°C). Allow to cool to 20°C, then add to the cold Greek yoghurt with the lime zest. Churn the yoghurt sorbet in the ice cream maker and immediately fill the 3D quenelle moulds. Chill before removing from the moulds for further use.

PASSIONFRUIT FOAM

Ingredients
140 g icing sugar
50 g albumen (dried egg-white powder)
250 g passionfruit purée with 10% sugar

Preparation
Mix the icing sugar and albumen, sift into the passion fruit juice and mix everything into a homogenous mixture. Beat with a mechanical beater into a light, foamy mass.
Place on silicone mats and dry for 6 hours in the food dryer at 65°C.

CITRUS GEL

Ingredients
125 g fresh lemon juice
125 g lime juice
250 g sugar water 1/1
25 g ginger syrup
7 g agar agar
5 g gellan gum

Preparation
Heat the lemon and lime juice together with the sugar water, ginger syrup and agar agar/ gellan mixture. Bring to the boil and then pour through a fine sieve. Cover and leave to cool completely. Mix the citrus gel smooth before use.

EXOTIC MANGO-PASSION-FRUIT-LIME COULIS

Ingredients
135 g sugar syrup 1/1
230 g mango purée with 10% sugar
150 g passionfruit purée with 10% sugar
10 g lime juice
5 g mango vinegar
1 g xanthan gum (cold binder)

Preparation
Mix the sugar syrup with the fruit purée and the mango vinegar. Then mix briefly with the xanthan gum to obtain a somewhat thicker (not runny) coulis.

MANGO BRUNOISE

Dice ripe mango into 3 mm cubes (brunoise) with a little exotic coulis.

FINISHING

Lime cress, flower petals
Exotic coulis

BART'S TIPS

It's not necessary to pre-crystallize the white chocolate for the exotic crispy-crunchy base, as the various ingredients need to be well-mixed into it. Then use as quickly as possible.

Praliné – chocolate – fruity caramel

Not the classic combination of praline and chocolate but one with a surprising addition of fruity caramel (mango-passionfruit), roughly-broken, roasted and caramelized hazelnuts and an exotic sorbet that gives the dessert the necessary acids.

HAZELNUT DACQUOISE

Ingredients
110 g almond broyage (50% caster sugar + 50% ground almond)
110 g fine-ground hazelnut powder
90 g flour
250 g egg white
210 g caster sugar

Yield: enough for two layers of biscuit, 40 × 30 cm

Preparation
Beat the egg white with the caster sugar till stiff but smooth, and add the sieved mixture of ground almonds, hazelnut powder and flour.
Spread evenly on the baking tray and bake for ten minutes at 200°C.

CRISPY LAYER (TO BE PLACED ON THE HAZELNUT DACQUOISE)

Ingredients
120 g melted milk chocolate
140 g fine hazelnut paste, unsugared
90 g feuilletine

Preparation
Mix the milk chocolate over a low heat with the hazelnut paste, and only then add the feuilletine.
Spread a thin, even layer on the dacquoise biscuit.
Then cut to the desired size (for dessert in the picture, a size of 2.5 cm × 14 cm was used).

MOUSSELINE PRALINÉ

Ingredients
200 g tempered butter
100 g hazelnut paste 50% (50% half-roasted hazelnuts + 50% caster sugar)
50 g fine hazelnut paste, unsugared
250 g Italian foam (cooking foam)

Preparation
Mix the tempered butter (at room temperature) with both hazelnut pastes and beat with the mechanical beater to a light mousseline.
Lastly fold the cooled Italian foam into the mousseline.

/// CONSTRUCTION ///

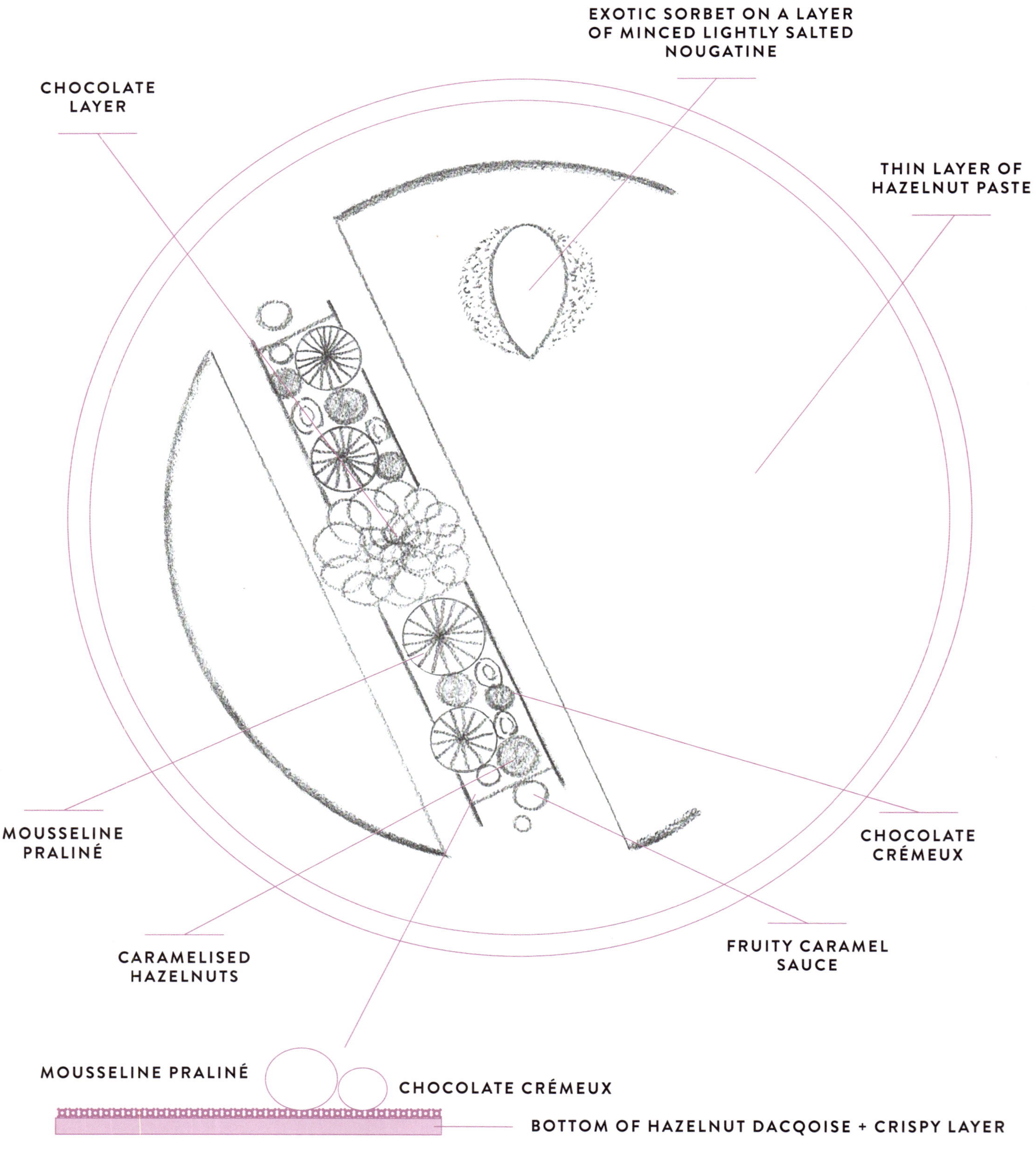

CHOCOLATE LAYER

EXOTIC SORBET ON A LAYER OF MINCED LIGHTLY SALTED NOUGATINE

THIN LAYER OF HAZELNUT PASTE

MOUSSELINE PRALINÉ

CARAMELISED HAZELNUTS

CHOCOLATE CRÉMEUX

FRUITY CARAMEL SAUCE

MOUSSELINE PRALINÉ

CHOCOLATE CRÉMEUX

BOTTOM OF HAZELNUT DACQOISE + CRISPY LAYER

ITALIAN FOAM

Ingredients
40 g water
150 g caster sugar
100 g egg white
15 g caster sugar

Preparation
Bring the water and most of the caster sugar gently to the boil.
Once the sugar syrup is boiling, beat together the egg whites and the caster sugar at medium speed.
Boil the sugar water to 121°C and then add it in an even jet to the firm but smoothly whipped egg whites.
Beat this 'Italian foam' at medium speed until cold.

LIGHTLY SALTED NOUGATINE

Ingredients
85 g water
35 g glucose
665 g caster sugar
415 g hazelnuts, peeled, broken and roasted
4 g coarse sea salt

Preparation
Make a caramel of the first three ingredients. For this, heat the water with the glucose and gradually add caster sugar to produce a caramel.
Immediately add the still warm roasted hazelnuts and the sea salt.
Spread the mix onto baking paper or a Silpat and allow to cool completely.
Break the nougatine to the desired size.

CHOCOLATE CRÉMEUX

Ingredients
100 g cream (35%)
100 g whole milk
20 g caster sugar
40 g egg yolks
105 g origin chocolate extra bitter 64%

Preparation
Heat the first four ingredients together to produce and anglaise (83°C) and add to the chocolate through a fine sieve. Mix everything to a smooth emulsion. Cover completely and allow to crystallize at 3°C. After cooling, the crémeux is smooth and pipeable.

FRUITY CARAMEL SAUCE

Ingredients
125 g mango purée
125 g passionfruit purée
juice of ½ lime
zest of 1½ lime
1 star of star anise
250 g caster sugar

Preparation
Bring the fruit juices to the boil and infuse the lime zest and star anise. Caramelize the caster sugar and quench gradually with the infused fruit juice (mango, passion, lime, lime zest and star anise).
Pour everything through a fine sieve into a plastic jar and leave to cool completely (3°C).

EXOTIC SORBET

Ingredients
260 g water
150 g caster sugar
80 g glucose powder
combined sorbet stabilizer
   (emulsifier and stabilizer)
300 g mango purée with 10% sugar
90 g passionfruit purée with
   10% sugar
60 g lime juice
40 g banana

Preparation
Heat the water to around 50°C and add to the mixture of caster sugar, atomized glucose and stabilizer.
Wait for half an hour (to allow the sugars to dissolve fully and for the stabilizer to bind lightly) before mixing the syrup with the mixed fruit juices. Check with a refractometer that the mixture is at 30°Brix (see also p. 24) and churn.
Place immediately into a 3D silicone quenelle mat.

FURTHER FINISHING

Praliné on plate technique: Place a small amount of praliné with a little neutral oil added onto the plate. Place the plate on a gramophone turntable, spin and rub with a wide brush on the plate until the desired distribution is obtained.
Chocolate decoration: see p. 28.
Thin slices of fondant chocolate and milk chocolate fan: see p. 33.

Scan the QR code or go to
www.lannoopublishinggroup.com/
desserts-video-en

Wild strawberry – coconut kaffir lime

A powerful combination of soft wild strawberry and crispy coconut dough, with the fresh acids of the kaffir lime and the cold coconut ice.

BASE OF THE DESSERT
(Reverse construction in a silicone mat, 7 cm diameter and 1 cm high)

1. COCONUT BUTTER DOUGH
Ingredients
125 g butter
60 g icing sugar
60 g grated coconut
50 g egg yolks
160 g flour
2 g coarse sea salt

Preparation
Mix the butter at room temperature with the icing sugar and grated coconut. When well mixed, add in the egg yolks and then fold in the sifted flour and salt to produce a homogeneous dough. Chill (3°C) before processing further. Roll out the chilled butter dough to 3 mm thick, prick, and press out the desired diameter. Sprinkle with egg and sprinkle with grated coconut for baking. Bake at 160°C for about 18 minutes until golden-brown.

2. CRÈME OF WILD STRAWBERRY AND RASPBERRY

Ingredients
165 g whole milk
½ vanilla stick
75 g caster sugar
100 g egg yolks
54 g gelatine (or 4½ gelatine leaves) (soaked)
150 g wild strawberry purée with 10% sugar
100 g raspberry purée with 10% sugar
250 g cream (35%)

Preparation
Heat the first four ingredients together to produce an anglaise (83°C) and then add to the soaked gelatine through a fine sieve.
Then stir in the mixture of fruit purées and add the 2/3 whipped cream at 25 to 30°C.

The structure and consistency of the crème determines at which temperature the cream is mixed in. This also depends on the intended purpose. For example, where it is intended for a pastry built up using the 'reverse construction' technique (as when using a more detailed silicon mat mould to obtain a more detailed shape), then the crème needs to be more fluid. In this case the cream is worked in at 30°C.
In a classical construction (for example in cake rings) it is advisable to use a thick, pipeable cream, giving better control during the construction process. In this case the cream is worked in at 25°C. Attention: this depends very much on the recipe, on the particular crème, and also on the proportions.

/// CONSTRUCTION ///

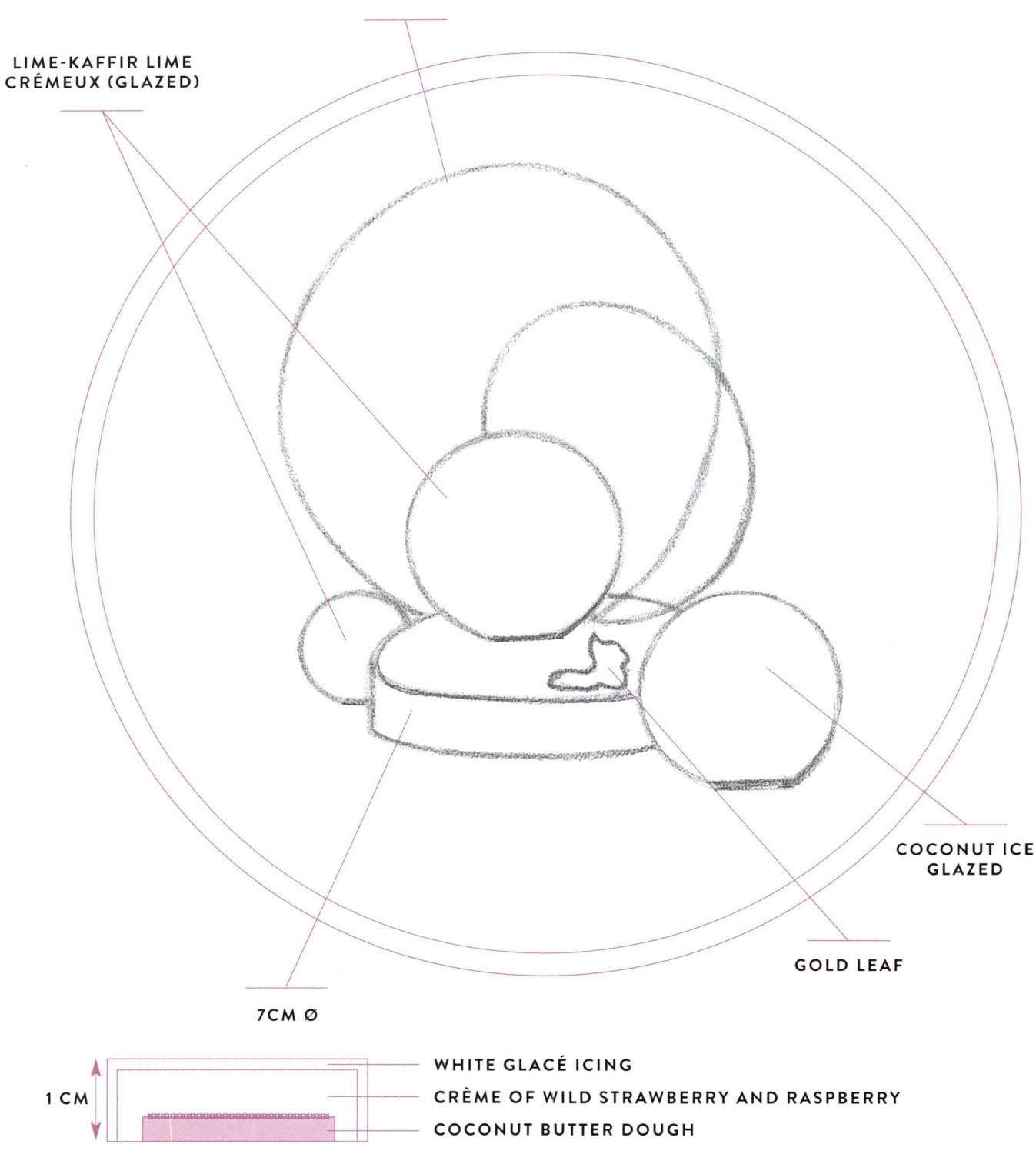

- ISOMALT DECORATION (GOLD RINGS)
- LIME-KAFFIR LIME CRÉMEUX (GLAZED)
- COCONUT ICE GLAZED
- GOLD LEAF
- 7CM Ø
- 1 CM
- WHITE GLACÉ ICING
- CRÈME OF WILD STRAWBERRY AND RASPBERRY
- COCONUT BUTTER DOUGH

LIME-KAFFIR LIME CRÉMEUX

Ingredients
255 g lime juice
grated zest of three kaffir limes
7 g kaffir lime leaves
195 g caster sugar
195 g eggs
21 g gelatine (or 3½ gelatine leaves)
150 g butter

Preparation
Bring the fresh lime juice to the boil, add the zest and leaves, cover with cling film and leave to infuse for fifteen minutes.
Pass the infused mixture through a fine sieve, and add to the yolks and caster sugar. Heat and stir to produce an anglaise (83°C). Add this through a sieve to the soaked gelatine. Allow to cool to 38°C before adding the soft butter to give a smooth emulsion.
Spoon the lime-kaffir lime crémeux into a 3D ball mat. Freeze.

COCONUT ICE

Ingredients
130 g caster sugar
25 g glucose powder
30 g skimmed milk powder
stabilizer
500 g coconut milk
135 g cream (35%)
60 g grated coconut (roasted)
30 g coconut liqueur

Preparation
Mix the dry ingredients (caster sugar, glucose powder, skimmed milk powder, stabilizer). Heat the coconut milk and cream to 60°C and stir in the mixed dry ingredients.
Pass through a fine sieve and mix the ice homogeneously (homogenizing).
Then leave to cool for 12 hours at 3°C (ripening process).
Churn the ice mix. Half-way through the churning add the roasted, fully chilled grated coconut.
Add the coconut liqueur just before the end of the churning.
Immediately fill the 3D silicone ball moulds and freeze.

WHITE GLACÉ ICING

Ingredients
225 g whole milk
225 g glucose
310 g white chocolate callets
white powder colouring
66 g gelatine (or 5½ gelatine leaves)
8 g titanium dioxide (white powder colouring E 171)
95 g neutral oil (grape seed oil, sunflower oil)

Preparation
Bring the whole milk and glucose to the boil and add to the white chocolate callets and white powder colouring.
Add the soaked gelatine when the chocolate is completely mixed. Then add the neutral oil.
Lastly mix the glacé icing to a homogeneous mass and pass through a fine sieve. Cover with cling film and store at 3°C until completely crystallized.
Heat the glacé chocolate to 35°C before fully glazing the prepared moulds (-20°C).

FURTHER FINISHING
Isomalt decoration (gold rings) – technique on p. 27
Gold leaf

BART'S TIPS

In the photo we've opted for a very simple presentation, but it's very nice to add wild strawberries and a little grated combava (kaffir lime zest).

Chocolate flan – pear – caramel

A dessert of soft chocolate flan in combination with salted caramel, crisp sesame nougatine, texture of pear and gianduja crème.

CHOCOLATE FLAN

1. CHOCOLATE BUTTER DOUGH
Ingredients
250 g butter (at room temperature)
2 g vanilla essence
65 g almond powder
165 g icing sugar
95 g egg yolks
435 g flour
30 g cocoa powder
3 g fleur de sel

Preparation
Mix the butter into the vanilla, almond powder and icing sugar using the beater spatula. Once homogenous, add the egg yolks. Lastly, sift and fold in the mixed flour, cocoa powder and salt just long enough to create homogeneous dough. Chill (3°C) before processing further. Roll out the chocolate butter dough on the desired baking tray and press out using the desired baking mould (square or rectangular). Place the butter dough in the baking mould and remove the dough round it.
Bake these butter dough bases in advance at 160°C for 8 minutes (half pre-baked).

2. CHOCOLATE FLAN
Ingredients
150 g whole milk
355 g cream (35%)
95 g eggs
425 g fondant chocolate

Preparation
Heat the first three ingredients with a Thermomix to 70°C (position 4) and then add the fondant chocolate. Mix/emulsify.
Fill the pre-baked bottoms with the chocolate flan up to a depth of 12 mm and bake for another 15 minutes at 150°C.
Wait until fully cooled before cutting the cholocate flan to the desired shape.

SALTED CARAMEL

Ingredients
15 g glucose
180 g caster sugar
300 g cream (35%)
70 g butter
2 g coarse sea salt

Preparation
Make a caramel of glucose and caster sugar and quench progressively with the hot mix of cream, butter and coarse sea salt (90°C).
Pass through a fine sieve and leave to cool.

HAZELNUT SPONGE CAKE

Ingredients
60 g caster sugar
40 g flour
125 g egg white
80 g egg yolks
80 g hazelnut paste 100%

Preparation
Mix the caster sugar with the flour. Then, using the Thermomix, mix in the egg whites, yolks and the hazelnut paste to produce a fine, homogeneous mass.

/// CONSTRUCTION ///

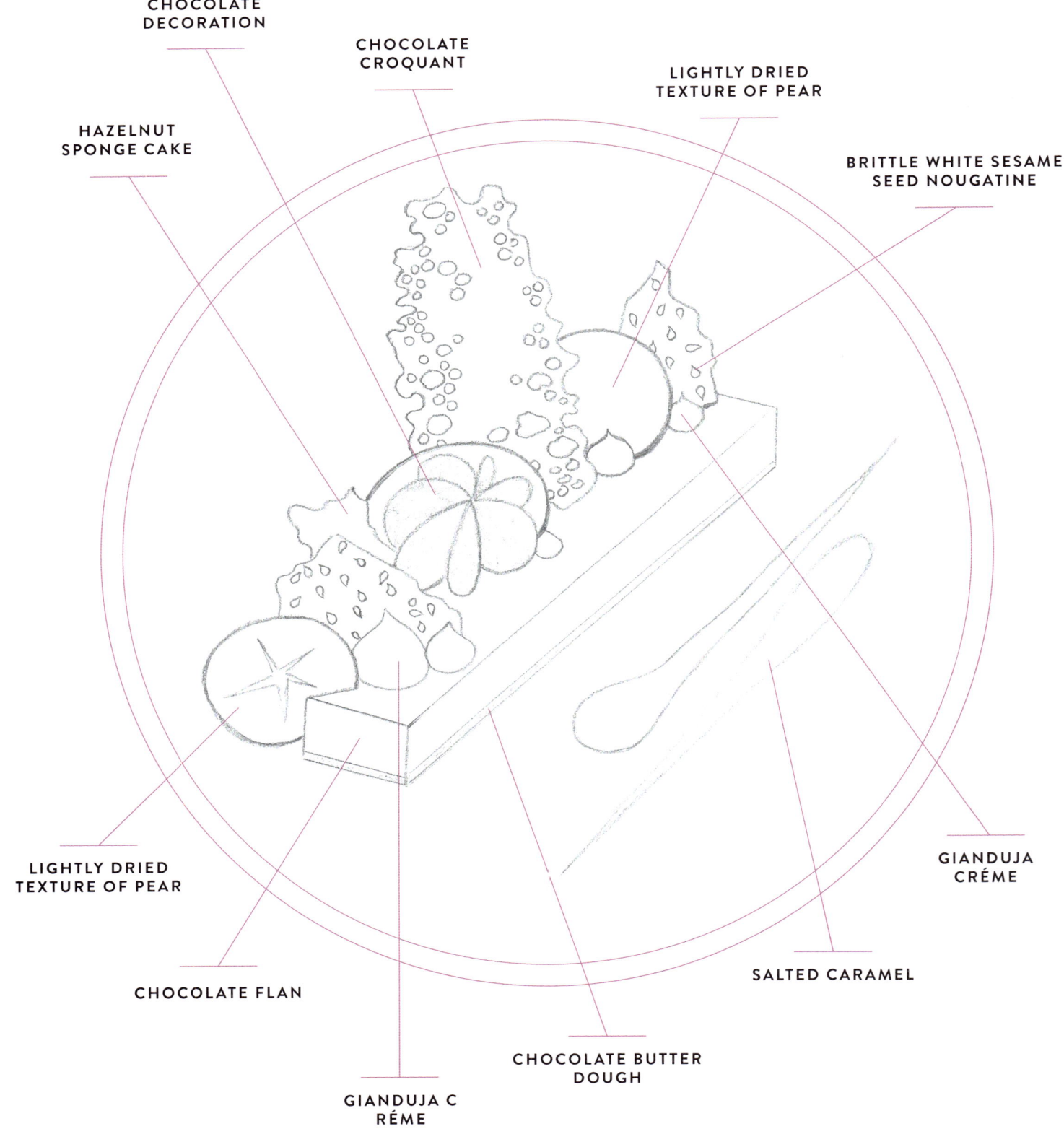

- CHOCOLATE DECORATION
- CHOCOLATE CROQUANT
- LIGHTLY DRIED TEXTURE OF PEAR
- HAZELNUT SPONGE CAKE
- BRITTLE WHITE SESAME SEED NOUGATINE
- LIGHTLY DRIED TEXTURE OF PEAR
- CHOCOLATE FLAN
- GIANDUJA CRÉME
- SALTED CARAMEL
- CHOCOLATE BUTTER DOUGH
- GIANDUJA CRÉME

Place in a siphon bottle, together with a few gas cartridges (N2O). Mix the mass with the gas by shaking the siphon bottle hard (good gas distribution).
Fill the isomo (insulating foam) cups half-full with the frothy mass and bake for about twenty seconds in a powerful microwave oven. After baking, turn the cups upside down immediately onto baking paper to avoid drying out.

BRITTLE WHITE SESAME SEED NOUGATINE

Ingredients
100 g glucose
135 g caster sugar
1.5 g coarse sea salt
100 g almond shavings
80 g white sesame seed

Preparation
Caramelize the glucose with the caster sugar and mix with the sea salt, lightly roasted almond shavings and sesame seeds.
Roll out as fast and as thin as possible (1 mm) between silicone mats. Leave to cool completely for further use. Store in a well-sealed container with a few bags of 'moisture absorbers'.

CHOCOLATE CROQUANT

Ingredients
175 g glucose
50 g fondant sugar
175 g isomalt
200 g fondant sugar
100 g bitter chocolate (80% cocoa)

Preparation
Boil the first 3 ingredients to 155°C. Add the second quantity of fondant sugar and boil again to 140°C. Then mix in the bitter chocolate and roll out thinly (about 3 mm) between two sheets of baking paper. Once fully cooled, mix the powder and place it on the Silpat baking mat using a fine sieve. Allow to melt in the oven at 150°C and allow to cool completely for further use.

LIGHTLY DRIED TEXTURE OF PEAR

Cut the unpeeled pear (conference) into thin slices with the mandoline slicer. Coat the pear slices with a mixture of sugar syrup and lime juice. Dry these slices for a few hours in the food dryer at 55°C. You can also use thin slices of fresh pear.

GIANDUJA CRÉME

Ingredients
200 g whole milk
60 g egg yolks
10 g caster sugar
24 g gelatine (or 2 gelatine leaves)
35 g milk chocolate (40%)
265 g gianduja hazelnut

Preparation
Prepare an anglaise (83°C) of whole milk, egg yolks and caster sugar. Pass through a fine sieve immediately and pour, in three rounds, into the chopped milk chocolate and gianduja mixture. Mix the whole into an emulsion and cool before use (3°C).
Stir the crémeux smooth and apply pretty 'tops' with a smooth spray nozzle.

FURTHER FINISHING

Chocolate decoration: technique chocolate circles see p. 31.

Desserts with fruit and chocolate /// 115

Mascarpone – orange – elderflower

A fresh, light dessert with orange and airy mascarpone in the lead role, with textures of white chocolate crunch with grated orange zest, orange crumble, orange ice cream and the fruity-sour touch of elderflower.

PREPARATION OF THE LIGHT MASCARPONE MOUSSE

Ingredients
Italian foam (cooking foam)
80 g water
300 g caster sugar
200 g egg white
30 g caster sugar

Preparation
Bring the water and most of the caster sugar gently to the boil.
Meanwhile, beat the egg whites with a small amount of the caster sugar at medium speed till stiff and smooth.
Boil the sugar water to 121°C. Then add in a uniform jet to the egg whites.
Beat this 'Italian foam' at medium speed until cold.

LIGHT MOUSSE OF MASCARPONE AND LEMON

Ingredients
30 g gelatine (or 2½ gelatine leaves)
150 g cooking foam
50 g lemon juice
250 g mascarpone
1 vanilla stick
100 g cream (35%)

Preparation
Add the soaked and melted gelatine to the lukewarm cooking foam and mix well. Then add and mix in the lemon juice. Stir lightly into the already mixed mascarpone, scraped-out vanilla stick and liquid cream.
Place at once into the selected silicone mats and freeze for further use.
Once cool, spray with a chocolate spray (100 g white chocolate mixed with 100 g liquid cocoa butter and a little yellow powder colouring) to create a yellow velvety layer on top of the airy mascarpone mousse.

ORANGE CRUMBLE

Ingredients
125 g butter
125 g caster sugar
110 g almond powder (100%)
grated zest of 1 orange
110 g flour
2 g salt
75 g feuilletine

Preparation
Mix the tempered butter at room temperature with the caster sugar, almond powder and grated orange zest. Fold in the sifted flour with the salt to produce a homogeneous dough.
Lastly distribute the feuilletine into the butter dough.
Bake at 150°C. During baking, mix the crumble to produce an optimum and evenly baked golden-brown colour.
Allow to cool completely before cutting/mixing the crumble.

/// CONSTRUCTION ///

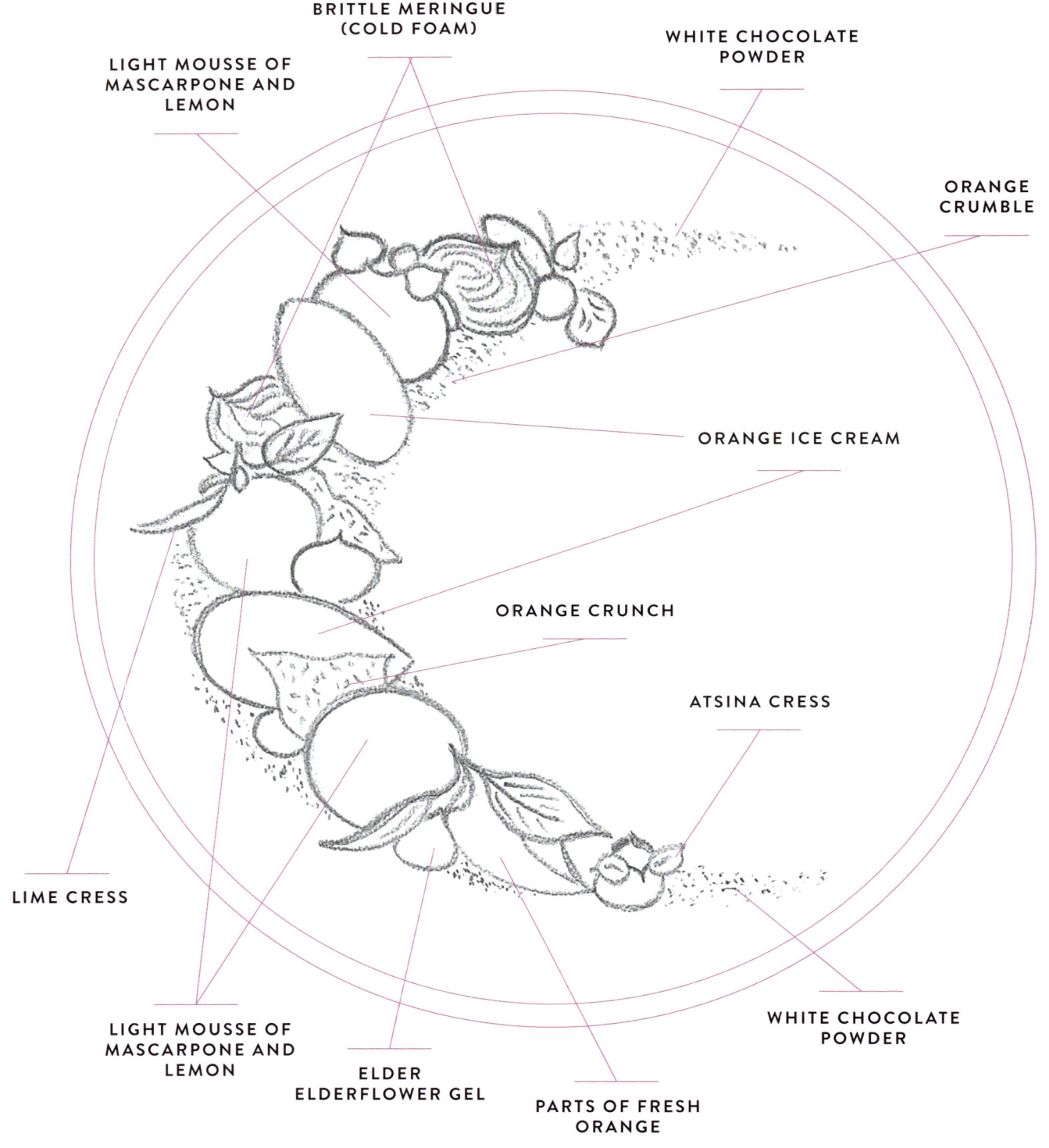

ORANGE ICE CREAM

Ingredients
200 g whole milk
100 g whipped cream
40 g skimmed milk powder
100 g caster sugar
50 g glucose powder
stabilizer
40 g egg yolks
425 g fresh orange juice
20 g concentrated orange juice

Preparation
Mix all the dry ingredients (skimmed milk powder, caster sugar, glucose powder, stabilizer). Heat the whole milk and whipped cream to 40°C and add in the dry ingredients. Add in also the egg whites, loosely beaten with a little milk or whipped cream.
Heat to a produce an anglaise (83°C), then pass through a fine sieve and add the fresh and concentrated orange juice. Mix the ice for 2 minutes (homogenizing, see also p. 19).
Place the ice mix for 12 hours in the refrigerator, then churn and place immediately into the desired moulds (3D quenelle shapes).

WHITE CHOCOLATE POWDER

Ingredients
50 g malto (Texturas)
100 g melted white chocolate

Preparation
Mix the malto with the molten white chocolate covering until a smooth powder is formed. Keep fresh in an airtight container.

BRITTLE MERINGUE (COLD FOAM)

Ingredients
200 g egg white
200 g caster sugar
180 g icing sugar

Preparation
Beat the egg white with the caster sugar into a firm but smooth foam. Then slowly fold in the sifted icing sugar. Using a toothed nozzle, pipe little whirls onto a baking tray with a silicone mat and bake for two hours at 90°C.

ORANGE CRUNCH

Ingredients
Rice crispies
white chocolate
orange zest

Preparation
p. 30

ELDERFLOWER GEL

Ingredients
300 g elderflower syrup
95 g water
4 g agar agar

Preparation
Add all ingredients together and bring to the boil. Pass through a fine sieve, cover and leave to chill.
Mix till smooth, eventually pushing it through a very fine sieve to produce a 'smooth gel'.

FINISHING

Little chunks of orange 'pealed alive'
Atsina cress, lime cress

Chocolate – whipped cream with kirsch slightly sour cherry

A dessert based on the incredible, world-famous Schwarzwälderkirschtorte (Black Forest gâteau). It's a real challenge to combine the different flavours and textures of chocolate, cream, kirsch and slightly sour cherries into a great whole ...

CHOCOLATE CREAM SPIRAL

Ingredients
250 g whole milk
150 g fondant chocolate
100 g gianduja
48 g gelatine (or 4 gelatine leaves)
500 g cream (35%)

Preparation
Boil the milk and pour it into the mix of fondant chocolate and gianduja. Mix to a homogenous mass. Soak and melt the gelatine and mix in well.
Heat to 27°C and lightly fold in the 2/3 whipped cream (at this temperature a smooth pipeable crème will develop).
Using a piping bag with a fine decoration nozzle, pipe the chocolate crème into a nice spiral on a plastic glazing sheet (rhodoid plastic for chocolate decorations) with the help of a gramophone turntable. Chill well before removing the plastic sheet.
Finish the chocolate cream by spraying with a chocolate spray mix (50% fondant chocolate + 50% cocoa butter and a little red powder colouring).
Place on a plate immediately.

LIGHTLY BOUND SOUR CHERRIES

Ingredients
350 g sour cherry purée with 10% sugar
90 g caster sugar
600 g sour cherries (griottes)
25 g cherry juice
15 g potato starch

Preparation
Heat the cherry purée with the caster sugar. Before reaching boiling point, add the sour cherries. Heat further and, just before boiling point, add the mixture of sour cherry juice and potato starch. Stir until light binding occurs. Cover and leave to chill completely in the refrigerator.

WHIPPED CREAM CRÈME

Ingredients
375 g whipped cream (40%)
½ vanilla stick
30 g icing sugar
25 g Schwarzwälder kirsch 40%

Preparation
Pre-mix all ingredients and store in the refrigerator. Take out and beat to the required stiffness (at medium speed). Apply drops of whipped cream using a smooth piping nozzle.

/// CONSTRUCTION ///

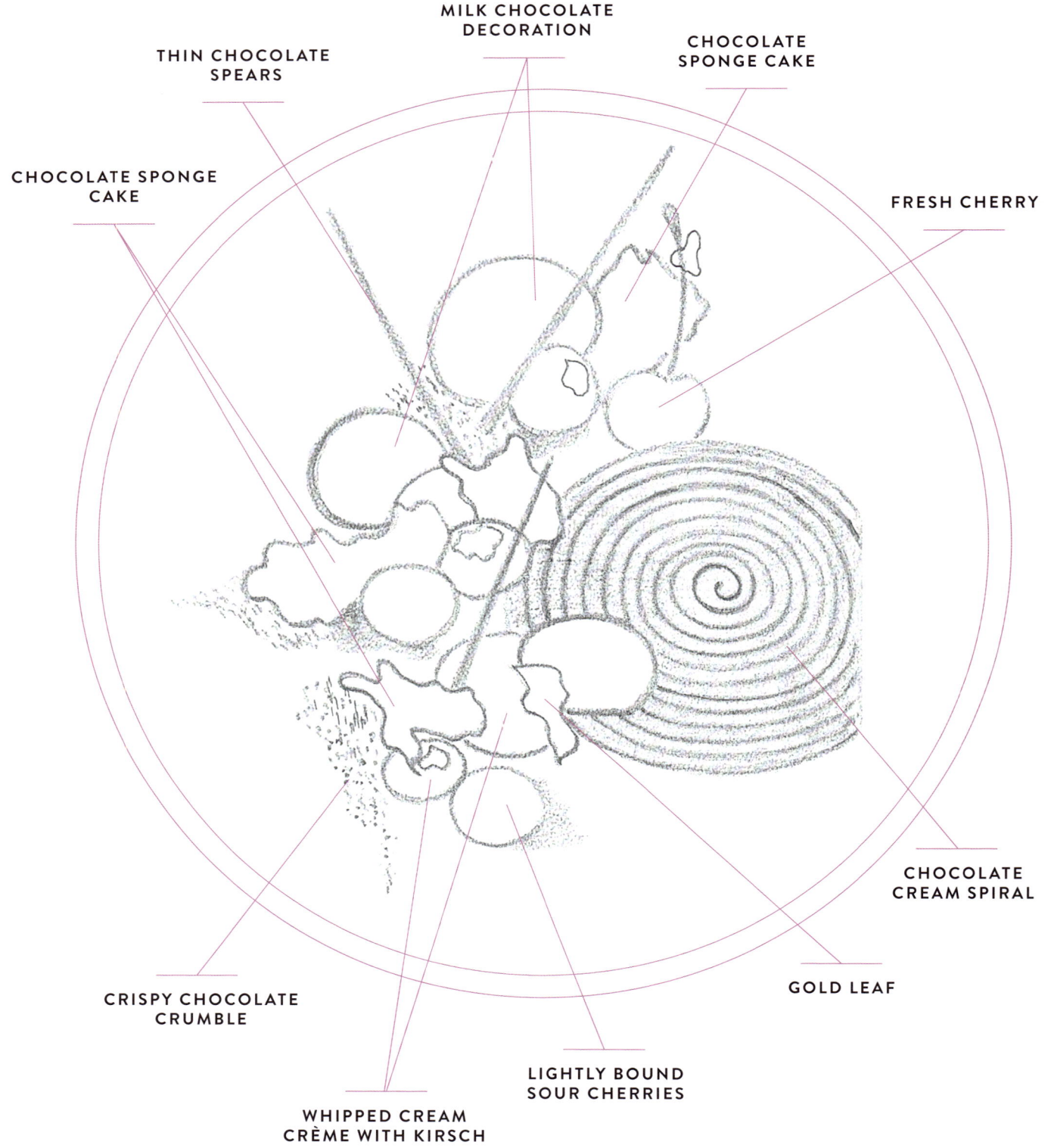

CHOCOLATE SPONGE CAKE

Ingredients

125 g almond powder 100%
125 g icing sugar
15 g flour
10 g cocoa powder
15 g of neutral olive oil or grape seed oil
2 g vanilla essence
165 g egg white
100 g egg yolks

Preparation
Mix all ingredients finely with a Thermomix and rub through a fine sieve. Then place the mixture into a siphon spray, add some gas cartridges (N2O) and mix into the mixture by shaking the siphon bottle hard (good gas distribution).
Fill the isomo (insulating foam) cups half-full with the frothy mass and bake for about twenty seconds in a powerful microwave oven. After baking, turn the cups upside down at once onto baking paper to avoid drying out.

EDIBLE BOTTOM OF THE BLACK FOREST GÂTEAU (CRISPY CHOCOLATE CRUMBLE)

Ingredients

100 g butter
100 g almond powder 100%
100 g soft brown sugar
90 g flour
15 g cocoa powder
2.5 g fleur de sel

Preparation
Chop the cold butter into cubes and immediately add the almond powder and the brown sugar.
Make a mixture of flour, cocoa powder and fleur de sel and fold lightly into the butter-almond-brown sugar sugar mixture.
Crumble the mass and bake on a Silpat baking mat at 150°C. Mix everything well during baking process to ensure an even bake and crispy crumble.
Mix this crumble very briefly after it has completely chilled and keep away from moisture in a dry, airtight container.

FINISHING AND PRESENTATION

Thin chocolate shavings (technique p. 31)
Thin chocolate spears (technique p. 29)
Fresh cherry
Gold leaf

Scan the QR code or go to
www.lannoopublishinggroup.com/
desserts-video-en

BART'S TIPS

By using a discarded gramophone turntable – one that can still turn – you get a different presentation of the chocolate crème.

Vanilla – red fruits hibiscus rose hip – lemongrass

A delicious vanilla ice cream with a fresh sour soup of hibiscus, rose hip and lemongrass, flanked with a crisp, slightly salty cookie and many red fruit textures.

VANILLA ICE CREAM

Ingredients
1 litre whole milk
400 g whipped cream
1 vanilla stick
120 g egg yolks
235 g caster sugar
90 g glucose powder
70 g skimmed milk powder
stabilizer (ensures better stability and shelf life of the ice cream, amount dependent on the brand)

Preparation
Mix the warm milk (60°C) with the whipped cream and the cut and scraped vanilla stick. Mix the dry ingredients (caster sugar, glucose powder, skimmed milk powder, stabilizer) and add to the milk.
Beat the egg yolks loosely, mix with some of the lukewarm mixture (milk, whipped cream and dry ingredients) and add back to the whole.
Continue to heat to produce an anglaise (83°C). Pass the composition immediately through a fine sieve and mix for 2 minutes (emulsifying / homogenizing). Let the ice cream mix chill down quickly and place it in the refrigerator (ripening process) for 12 hours.

Churn the vanilla ice cream and place in a 3D ball mat (4 cm diameter balls).

COLD SYRUP OF HIBISCUS-ROSEHIP AND LEMONGRASS

Ingredients
300 g water
80 g caster sugar
30 g of dried hibiscus-rosehip (dried loose tea)
2 stalks of lemongrass
15 g lime juice
zest of 2 limes

Preparation
Heat the water with the sugar to 90°C and add the mixture of dried hibiscus-rosehip, sliced pieces of lemongrass, lime juice and lime zest.
Cover with cling film and leave to infuse for thirty minutes.
Pour through a fine sieve and leave the syrup to chill in the refrigerator.
Wait till chilled to 3°C before using.

SABLE BRETON COOKIE (SHORTBREAD BISCUIT WITH SLIGHTLY SALTY TOUCH)

Ingredients
280 g butter (at room temperature)
2 g vanilla essence
280 g caster sugar
140 g egg yolks
390 g flour
10 g baking powder
5 g coarse sea salt

Preparation
Mix the butter smoothly with the vanilla essence, caster sugar and egg yolks. Add the sifted mixture of flour, baking powder and coarse sea salt and mix briefly to a homogeneous dough. Chill (3°C) before processing further.
Roll out the chilled dough 2.5 mm thick and bake in an stainless steel mould of the desired size at 170°C for about 17 minutes.
Size of the cookie in the photo: 13.5 × 2.5 cm

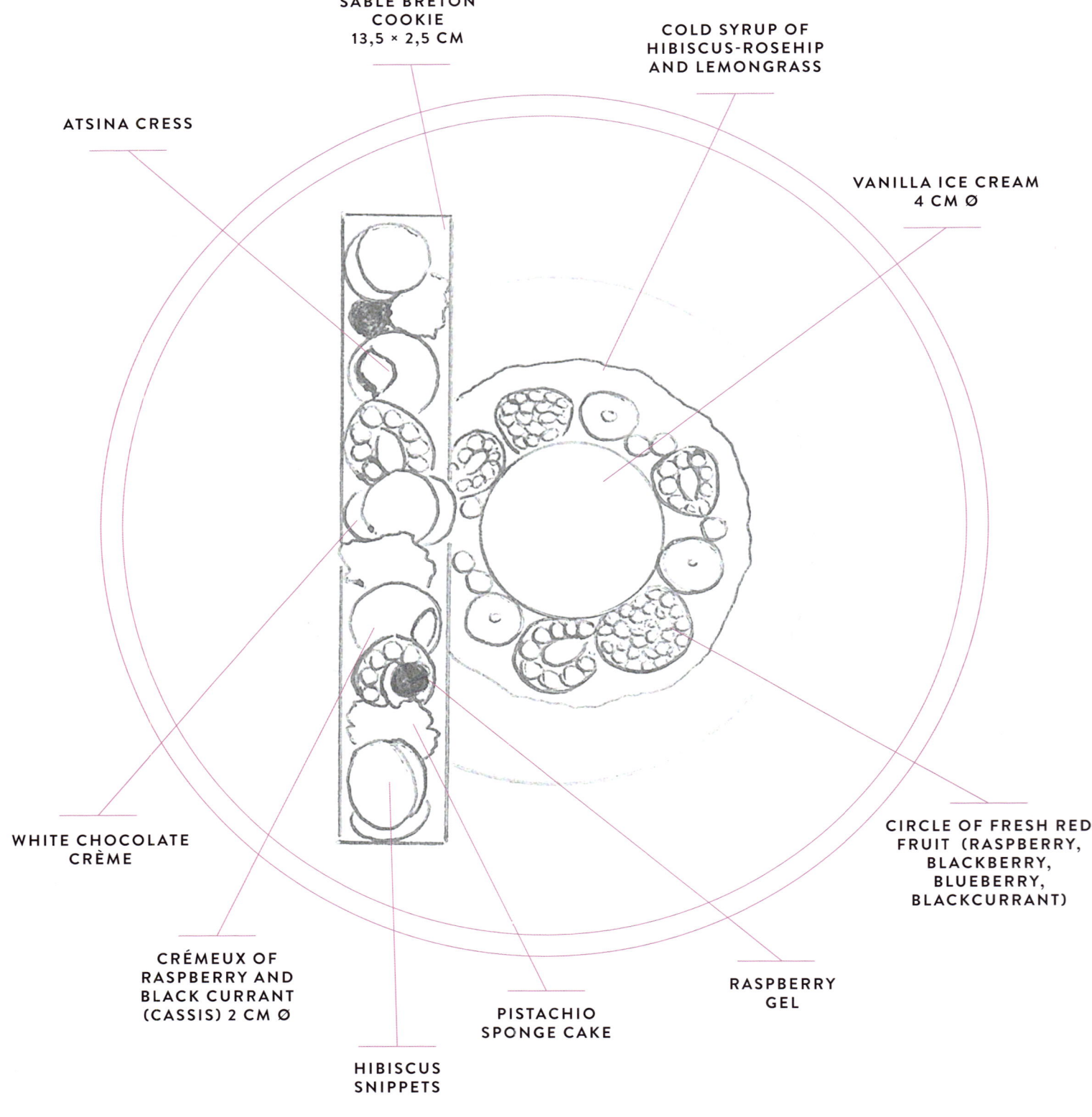

CRÉMEUX OF RASPBERRY AND BLACK CURRANT (CASSIS)

Ingredients
220 g raspberry purée with
   10% sugar
80 g blackcurrant purée with
   10% sugar
70 g caster sugar
120 g egg yolks
90 g eggs
36 g gelatine (or 3 gelatine leaves)
110 g butter

Preparation
Heat and stir the first five ingredients to produce an anglaise (83°C), and then add the soaked gelatine. Allow to cool to 38°C before adding the soft butter into the mass (crémeux).
Place the mixture into a 3D silicone ball mat (2 cm diameter balls) and cool before further use.
Finish the crémeux with a neutral glaze, with 15-20% raspberry purée added and a few drops of red liquid colouring. Heat and apply the glaçage at 50°C to guarantee a thin layer of glaze round the crémeux.

WHITE CHOCOLATE CRÈME (BEATABLE GANACHE)

Ingredients
160 g cream (35%)
½ vanilla stick
240 g white chocolate
12 g gelatine (or 1 gelatine leaf)
350 g cream (35%)

Preparation
Make a ganache from the smaller amount of cream, scraped vanilla stick and white chocolate. For this, heat the cream to 60°C, add the vanilla stick and soaked gelatine and mix through a fine sieve with the melted white chocolate. Only when all the chocolate is absorbed in the mass can the mixture be mixed into an emulsion.
Then add the rest of the liquid cream (3°C) and mix/emulsify again.
Cool the emulsion for at least 6 hours at 3°C. After this, the mixture can be beaten with the mechanical beater to the desired stiffness (smoothly pipeable).

PISTACHIO SPONGE CAKE

Ingredients
125 g pistachios, peeled
125 g icing sugar
25 g flour
165 g egg white
100 g egg yolks
15 g grape seed oil

Preparation
Mix the pistachios very fine with the Thermomix, then add the other dry ingredients (icing sugar and flour) and mix finely. Only then add the egg white, egg yolks and oil and mix for another sixty seconds at position 5.
Rub the mass through a fine sieve before placing in a spray siphon. Add some gas cartridges (N2O) and mix the gas into the mixture by shaking the siphon bottle hard (good gas distribution).
Fill the isomo (insulating foam) cups half-full with the frothy mass and bake for about twenty seconds in a powerful microwave oven. After baking, turn the cups upside down immediately onto baking paper to avoid drying out.

HIBISCUS SNIPPETS

Ingredients
150 g strong hibiscus tea (35 g hibiscus leaves in 250 g water)
100 g icing sugar
30 g albumin

Preparation
Pour hot water (90°C) onto the loose hibiscus leaves and leave to draw for fifteen minutes. Then pour through a very fine sieve and leave the strong infusion to cool in the refrigerator.
Mix the cold infused hibiscus tea with the mixture of icing sugar and albumin. Beat this with the mixer at medium speed to the desired firmness (airy and pipeable).
Place little hemispheres on silicone baking mats in the food drier and pour some minced dry freezed fruit. and leave to dry for six hours at 65°C.

RASPBERRY GEL

Ingredients
250 g raspberry purée with 10% sugar
70 g sugar water 1/1
2.5 g agar agar

Preparation
Boil the raspberry purée with the sugar water and agar agar, pass through a fine sieve and allow to cool/solidify completely.
Mix to a smooth gel, eventually passing it through a very fine sieve.

FINISHING
Raspberry, blackberry, blueberry, blackcurrant
Atsina cress

Scan the QR code or go to
www.lannoopublishinggroup.com/desserts-video-en

BART'S TIPS

Make the white chocolate crème a day in advance and store in the refrigerator. Then beat the crème with a mixer at medium speed. This gives you a maximum smooth structure.

Or if you want a thicker syrup of hibiscus, rosehip and lemongrass, boil 500 g of syrup with agar agar and leave to cool fully before using.

Coconut – lychee – yuzu – white chocolate

A delicious chocolate dessert with an exotic touch of coconut and lychee!
The taste of the different coconut textures (soft, fresh and crispy) is sharpened with a yuzu gel.

LONG NARROW PASTRY (INSIDE CHOCOLATE DECORATION/TUNNEL)

1. COCONUT DACQUOISE
Ingredients
125 g icing sugar
25 g almond powder 100%
100 g grated coconut
150 g egg white
50 g caster sugar

Preparation
Mix the icing sugar with the almond powder and grated coconut.
Beat the egg white firm but smooth with the caster sugar and fold it into the mixture.
Place 2 cm wide strips of the mixture on a wide baking plate and bake at 170°C for about 18 minutes.
After baking cut to the desired length.

2. COCONUT CRÈME
Ingredients
60 g gelatine (or 5 gelatine leaves)
375 g coconut purée with 10% sugar
300 g cream (35%)
25 g coconut liqueur

Preparation
Melt the soaked gelatine and add to the lukewarm coconut purée. As soon as this mass begins to gel (20-25°C), add the 2/3 whipped cream. Lastly, mix the coconut liqueur into the crème.
Place the coconut crème onto a Silpat baking mat and chill sufficiently to remove easily.

3. WHITE GLACÉ ICING
Ingredients
310 g white chocolate
4 g titanium dioxide (white powder colouring)
225 g whole milk
225 g glucose
66 g gelatine (or 5½ gelatine leaves)
95 g grape seed oil

Preparation
Mix the white chocolate and the titanium dioxide.
Heat the whole milk with the glucose to 80°C and add it gradually to the white chocolate and titanium dioxide until these are completely absorbed. Mix the soaked gelatine into the warm mass. Lastly, mix everything into an emulsion while adding grape seed oil.
Cover and leave to crystallize completely at 3°C (refrigerator).
Heat the glaze to 35°C and glaze the pre-prepared coconut crème (-20°C).

Glaze the coconut crème with the white chocolate-based glazing and place immediately on the cut-to-size coconut dacquoise.
The chocolate decoration can now be placed on top with the other flavours and textures.

/// CONSTRUCTION ///

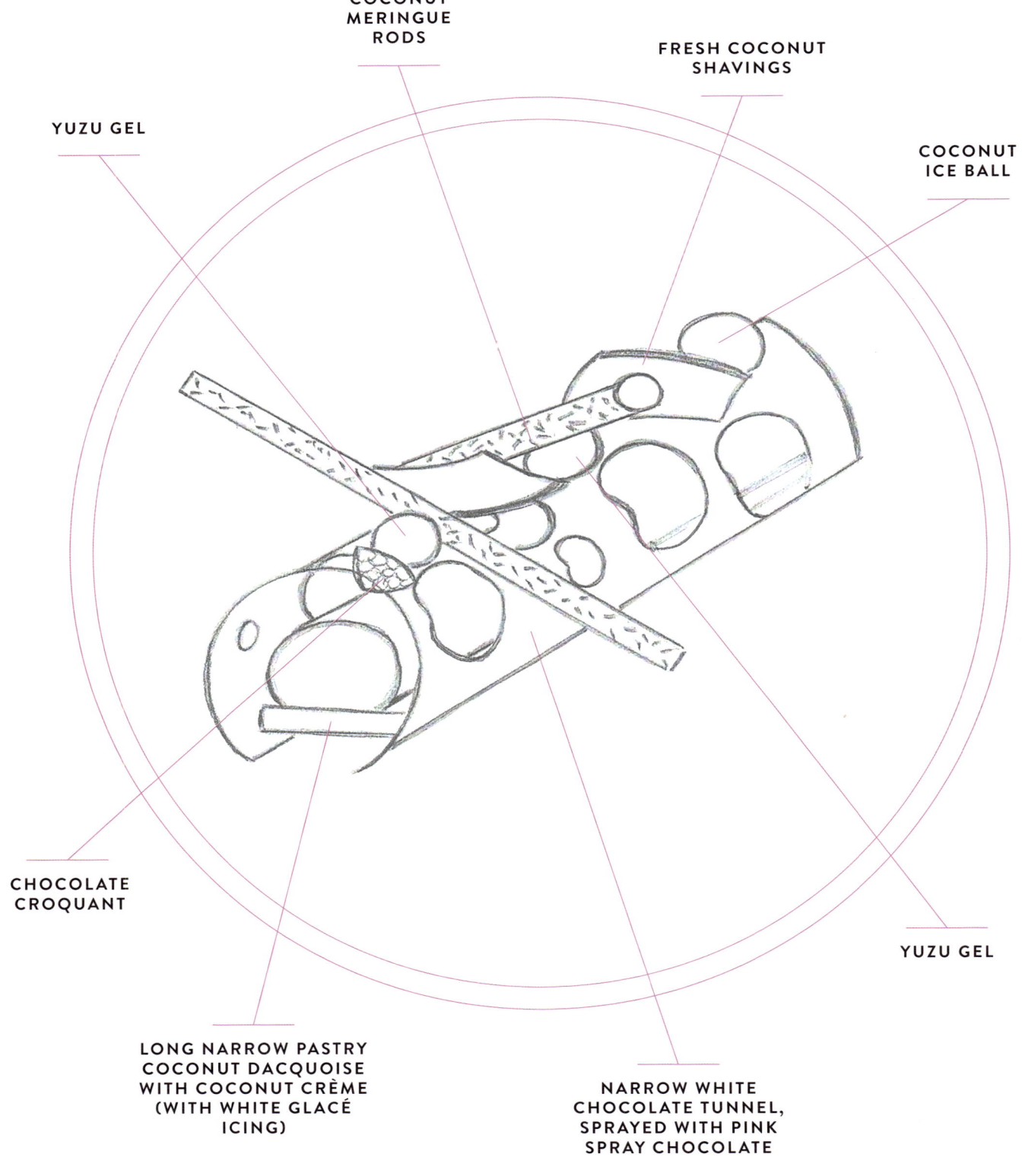

- COCONUT MERINGUE RODS
- FRESH COCONUT SHAVINGS
- YUZU GEL
- COCONUT ICE BALL
- YUZU GEL
- CHOCOLATE CROQUANT
- LONG NARROW PASTRY COCONUT DACQUOISE WITH COCONUT CRÈME (WITH WHITE GLACÉ ICING)
- NARROW WHITE CHOCOLATE TUNNEL, SPRAYED WITH PINK SPRAY CHOCOLATE

The following recipes are used for the chocolate decoration:

COCONUT ICE BALL

Ingredients
250 g coconut purée with 10% sugar
a little lime zest
0.5 g xanthan gum

Preparation
Mix the coconut purée with the lime zest and the cold binder. Distribute the mixture into a 3D ball mat with a ball diameter of no more than 1 cm (3 g). Serve frozen with the dessert.

YUZU GEL

Ingredients
100 g yuzu juice
110 g water
85 g caster sugar
9 g agar agar

Preparation
Mix all the ingredients and bring to the boil, stirring all the time, then pass through a fine sieve, cover and place in the refrigerator. Mix everything briefly before use, eventually passing through a sieve to obtain a shiny, smooth yuzu gel.

COCONUT MERINGUE RODS

Ingredients
250 g egg white
250 g caster sugar
225 g icing sugar

Preparation
Beat the egg white with the caster sugar to a firm but smooth mass, then slowly mix in the sifted icing sugar. Produce narrow rods of the desired length and sprinkle with grated coconut. Dry in an oven at 100°C for 2 hours. Once completely cooled, keep dry in an airtight container.

CHOCOLATE CROQUANT
Mix a little pre-crystallized white chocolate with rice crispies and roll out between two sheets of baking paper. Once fully hard, break into the desired pieces.

FURTHER DECORATION
Narrow white chocolate tunnel, 3 cm in diameter and 12 cm long, sprayed with pink spray chocolate. Chocolate decoration technique: see p. 31
Small fresh pieces of lychee
Fresh coconut shavings
Thin rods of coconut meringue

BART'S TIPS

The chocolate decoration demands a little more technique and work, but the final result is worth it. Aim for very thin-spread chocolate.

Panna cotta – lemon verbena – red fruit

White chocolate mascarpone panna cotta with red fruit and a very fresh lemon verbena juice. To give crunch, a caramel with sesame seeds is used.

ALMOND BISCUIT (BISCUIT JOCONDE)

Ingredients
250 g eggs
335 g almond broyage (50% ground almonds + 50% caster sugar)
45 g flour
180 g egg white
40 g caster sugar
40 g butter

Preparation
Beat the eggs with the coarsely sieved mixture of ground almond and flour until slightly frothy.
Lightly fold in the firmly but smoothly beaten egg white with the sugars.
Lastly mix the melted butter (40°C) into the biscuit and spread out on two 40 × 30 cm baking trays covered with a layer of baking paper.
Bake the almond biscuit at 230°C for around seven minutes. After baking, remove immediately from the baking tray.

WHITE CHOCOLATE MASCARPONE PANNA COTTA (3D PIES)

Ingredients
250 g whole milk
¾ vanilla stick
5 large lemon verbena leaves
42 g gelatine (or 3½ gelatine leaves)
200 g white chocolate
50 g mascarpone
260 g cream (35%)

Preparation
Bring the milk to the boil, add the scraped-out vanilla stick and lemon verbena and leave to infuse for fifteen minutes. Then pour the mixture through a fine sieve onto the soaked gelatine. Wait until the gelatine is absorbed optimally before mixing smoothly with the white chocolate covering (melted).
Add the mascarpone and mix the whole into a homogeneous mass (emulsion).
At 28°C, add the 2/3 whipped cream to the whole.

Transfer the chocolate-mascarpone panna cotta into a 3D cobblestone silicone mat and fill to half a centimetre below the edge. Finish with a layer of biscuit and freeze for further use.
After taking out of the mould, spray the finished shapes with a white chocolate spray mass. For this, mix 150 g of white covering chocolate with 150 g of liquid cocoa butter and spray with a spray gun and compressor onto the cold products (velvet effect).

RASPBERRY GEL

Ingredients
250 g raspberry purée with 10% sugar
70 g sugar water 1/1
2.5 g agar agar

Preparation
Boil the raspberry purée with the sugar water and agar agar. Pour through a fine sieve and allow to cool/coagulate completely before use.
Mix to a smooth gel, eventually rubbing through a very fine sieve.

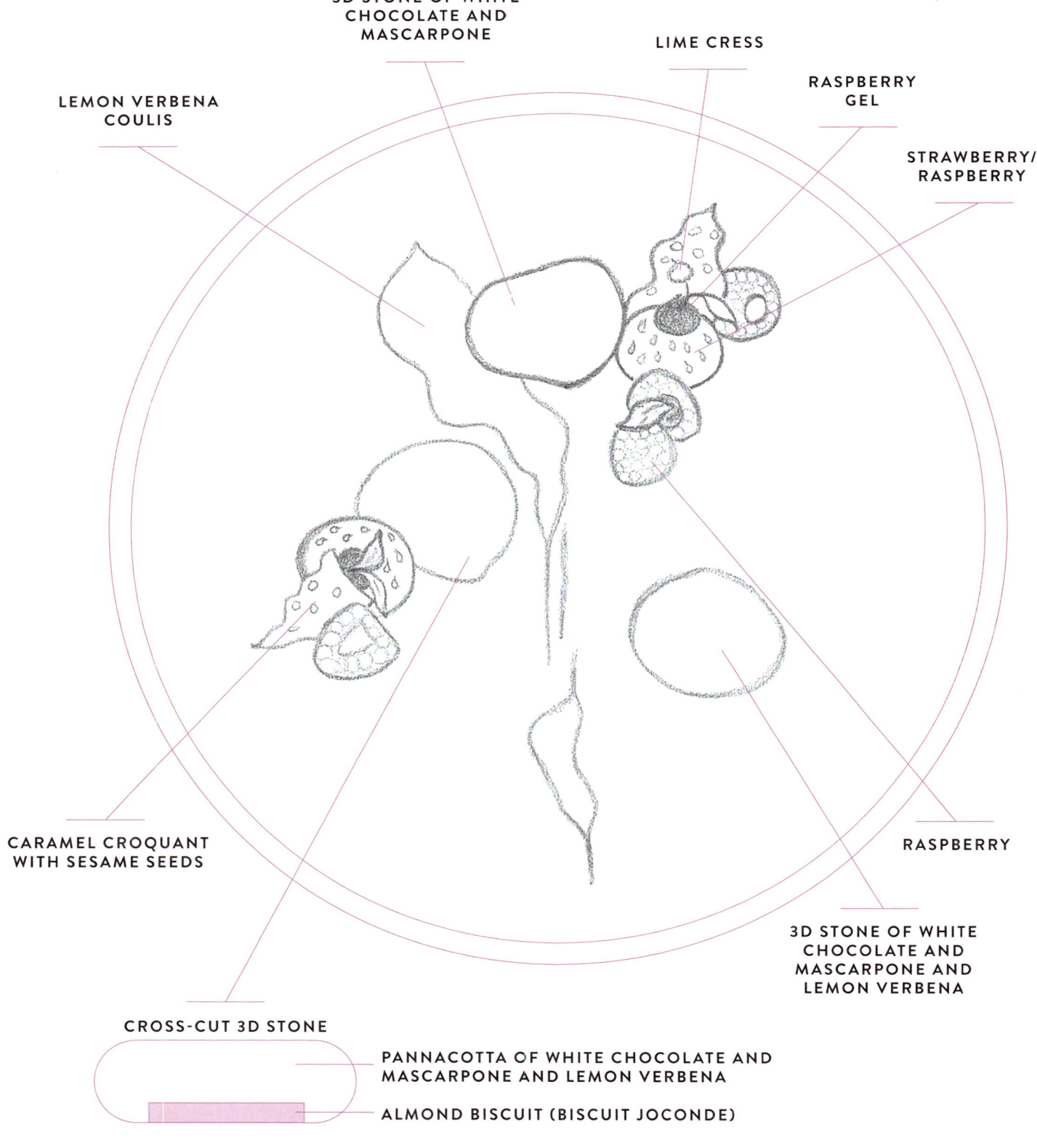

LEMON VERBENA COULIS

Ingredients
40 g fresh lemon verbena
65 g lime juice
40 g caster sugar
55 g neutral oil (e.g. grape seed oil, sunflower oil)

Preparation
Place the fresh lemon verbena in a small bowl and add the fresh lime juice, caster sugar and oil. Mix the whole to the desired fineness of the lemon verbena. If desired, add lime or sugar to taste.

CARAMEL CROQUANT WITH SESAME SEEDS

Ingredients
40 g whole milk
40 g glucose syrup
80 g butter
50 g caster sugar
2 g pectin
100 g sesame seeds
20 g flour

Preparation
Heat the whole milk, glucose syrup and butter together to 50°C. Stir in the mixed caster sugar and pectin. Bring gently to the boil for about 1 minute and remove from the heat. Immediately add the lightly roasted sesame seeds and the sifted flour.
Then roll out the resulting mass between baking paper to 1 mm thickness and freeze until further use.
Bake at 170°C for about fifteen minutes until a golden brown caramel colour is formed.
Allow to cool completely for optimum firmness and then break into pieces of the desired size.

FINISHING
Raspberry
Crossed raspberry-strawberry
Lime cress

BART'S TIPS

The lemon verbena coulis connects all the flavours of the dessert. Make sure the colour is thick enough and well bound.

Spiced chocolate – orange – buckthorn

This dessert consists of a lightly spiced chocolate crème combined with a crispy base. The orange crémeux comes on top of the chocolate crème as a second main flavour. All the other recipes are additions to the foregoing main tastes and provide textural variety, making the dessert a lot more fun and exciting.

RING OF LIGHTLY SPICED CHOCOLATE CRÈME CRISP BASE

Ingredients
100 g milk chocolate
200 g hazelnut paste 100%
50 g rice crispies
75 g feuilletine
35 g finely chopped cocoa kernels

Preparation
Mix the melted milk chocolate (40°C) with the hazelnut paste, and only then add the mixture of rice crispies, feuilletine and cocoa kernels. Immediately roll out the resulting mass 3 mm thick between baking paper and press out the desired shapes (in the dessert on the photo this is a ring of Ø 11 cm) once the chocolate has slightly crystallized (hardened). Chill for subsequent use (building the basic chocolate cake).

LIGHTLY SPICED CHOCOLATE CREAM

Ingredients
150 g whole milk
9 g fruit pepper (mix of pepper, coriander, aniseed, dried pieces of fruit, strawberry or blackberry)
35 g caster sugar
50 g egg yolks
360 g fondant chocolate
375 g cream (35%)

Preparation
Bring the milk to boil and infuse the fruit pepper in it for fifteen minutes. Pass the infused milk through a fine sieve, and add to the yolks and caster sugar. Heat and stir to produce an anglaise (83°C). Add the anglaise to the chocolate and emulsify (mix to a smooth emulsion).
At 30-32°C, mix in the 2/3 whipped cream to produce a smooth crème.
Place the lightly spiced chocolate crème into the selected silicone mould (ring) and finish with a pre-prepared crispy base. Press the base slightly into the cream.
Cool in the freezer for further processing/finishing (glazing).

PURPLE GLAZING

Ingredients
85 g water
150 g caster sugar
150 g glucose
150 g white chocolate callets
Purple powder colouring, fat-soluble
90 g gelatine (or 3½ gelatine leaves)
155 g sweet condensed milk
60 g neutral jelly
silver glitter powder

Preparation
Bring water, caster sugar and glucose slowly to the boil and gradually mix with the chocolate callets, purple powder colouring and soaked gelatine mass. When fully incorporated, mix the sweet condensed milk, neutral jelly and desired amount of silver glitter powder to a smooth, homogeneous mass.
Pass the glazing through a fine sieve and crystallize for 12 hours at 3°C (refrigerator).
Only then glaze the lightly spiced chocolate crème with the purple glazing, warmed to 30-35°C.
Turn out the glazed circle or ring of lightly spiced chocolate crème immediately onto the serving plate to decorate further.

/// CONSTRUCTION ///

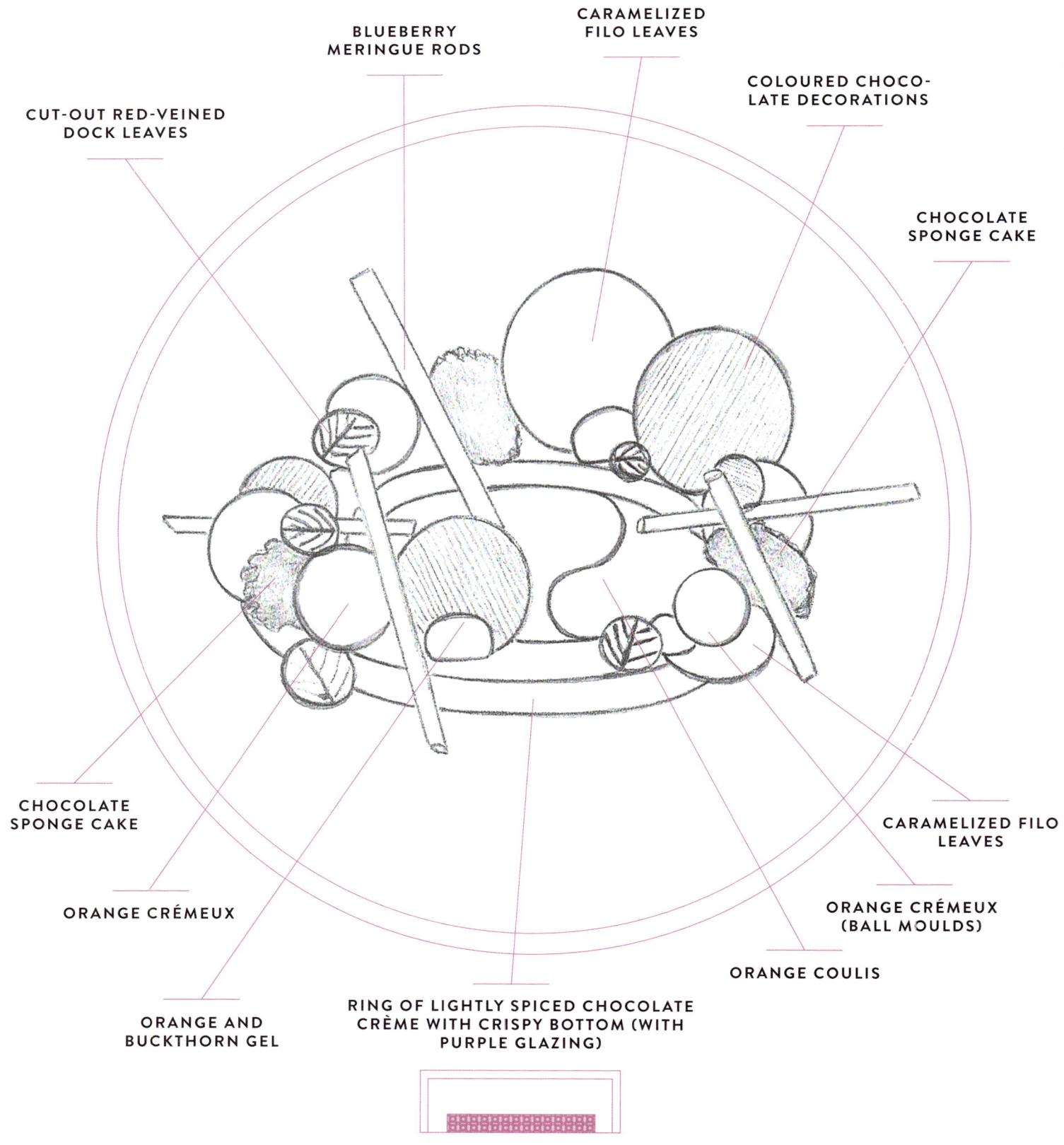

ORANGE CRÉMEUX (BALL MOULDS)

Ingredients
240 g whipped cream
45 g concentrated orange juice (freezer)
1 ½ orange zest
¼ vanilla stick
25 g caster sugar
50 g egg yolks
18 g gelatine (or 1½ gelatine leaves)
75 g butter

Preparation
Heat the first six ingredients together to produce an anglaise (83°C) and then add to the soaked gelatine through a fine sieve.
Allow to cool to 38°C before adding the soft butter to give a smooth emulsion. Place the orange crémeux in the 3D silicone ball moulds (2 cm diameter) and place in the freezer.
Remove the orange crémeux balls from the mould and glaze with a neutral jelly (50°C), flavoured and coloured with 10% concentrated orange juice and eventually little orange concentrate and orange colouring.

CHOCOLATE SPONGE CAKE

Ingredients
125 g almond powder 100%
125 g icing sugar
15 g flour
10 g cocoa powder
15 g neutral olive oil or grape seed oil
2 g vanilla essence
165 g egg white
100 g egg yolks

Preparation
Mix all the ingredients in a Thermomix and rub the mass through a fine sieve before placing in a spray siphon. Then add some gas cartridges (N2O) and mix the gas into the mixture by shaking the siphon bottle hard (good gas distribution).
Fill the isomo (insulating foam) cups half-full with the frothy mass and bake for about twenty seconds in a powerful microwave oven. After baking, turn the cups upside down immediately onto baking paper to avoid drying out.

BLUEBERRY MERINGUE RODS

Ingredients
125 g icing sugar
40 g albumin
250 g blueberry purée with 10% sugar

Preparation
Make a mixture of sifted icing sugar and albumin and add the blueberry purée. Then beat at medium speed into a light, pipeable meringue.
Prepare narrow rods of the desired length and dry in a drying tower (food drier) at 65°C for six hours.

ORANGE AND BUCKTHORN GEL

Ingredients
30 g caster sugar
3 g agar agar
250 g fresh orange juice
100 g buckthorn juice

Preparation
Mix the caster sugar with the agar agar and add to the orange juice-buckthorn mixture. Bring to the boil for 30 seconds, pass through a fine sieve and keep covered in the refrigerator.
Before use, this gel should be 'turned smooth' by briefly mixing before placing it in an icing bag or a dispenser.

CARAMELIZED FILO LEAVES (CRISP SPRING ROLL PASTRY)

Ingredients
1 sheet filo pastry
10 g butter
15 g caster sugar

Preparation
Brush the filo sheets thinly with a layer of melted butter and sprinkle evenly with fine caster sugar. Press or cut the filo sheets to the desired size and bake between two silicone baking mats at 170°C. Leave to cool completely, and eventually break into pieces for decorating.

THIN CIRCLES OF COLOURED CHOCOLATE DECORATIONS
See chocolate decorations on p. 33

ORANGE COULIS

Ingredients
1 clove
1 star of star anise
½ vanilla stick
300 g fresh orange juice
110 g caster sugar
1 g agar agar
10 g Mandarine Napoléon

Preparation
First infuse the herbs in the fresh orange juice. Then prepare a caramel with the caster sugar and quench with the hot, infused orange juice. Bring the resulting mixture to the boil again with the agar agar and pass through a fine sieve. Leave to cool slightly, add the Mandarine Napoléon, allow to cool further, cover, and place in the refrigerator.

FOR THE SPICED ORANGE PEARLS
Bind the resulting orange coulis with gelatine (1 leaf/ 100 g coulis) and distribute in a diameter 3D silicone mould (small ball shapes. Freeze, then remove for further use.
Finish with cut-out red-veined dock leaves and lime cress.

FINISHING
Red-veined dock leaves
Lime cress

BART'S TIPS

Glaze the lightly spiced chocolate crème immediately with the purple glitter glaze. Do this straight out of the freezer. In this way you get a thin layer and a good adhesion. Finish directly on the serving plate (defrosts very quickly because of its thickness of 12 mm).
The addition of orange juice to the buckthorn juice gives the gel a more pleasant, milder sour fruit flavour.

Sour cherry clafoutis – peach – rosemary

A delicious clafoutis of sour cherry, combined with red fruit on an airy white chocolate-vanilla crème and a peach sorbet scented with rosemary.

SHORTBREAD BASE

Ingredients
250 g butter
165 g icing sugar
2 g vanilla powder (100% vanilla stick)
65 g almond powder (100%)
95 g egg yolks
470 g flour
2 g coarse sea salt

Preparation
Add the butter at room temperature with the icing sugar, almond powder and vanilla powder. When well mixed, add the egg yolks. Lastly, fold in the sifted mixture of flour and sea salt to produce a homogeneous dough.
Chill the butter dough to 3°C for further processing.
Roll out the chilled butter dough to 2.5 mm thick, prick, and press out the desired diameter (6 cm). Pre-heat the oven to 170°C and half-bake the dough in rings covered with baking paper.
Do not remove the baking rings after baking: the pre-baked butter dough now adheres sufficiently to the ring that the liquid clafoutis filling will not flow out during the second baking.

CLAFOUTIS FILLING

Ingredients
100 g eggs
50 g caster sugar
15 g flour
300 g sour cream
30 g passion fruit purée with 10% sugar

Preparation
Beat the eggs lightly and mix with the mixture of caster sugar and flour. Add the mixture of sour cream and passion fruit purée.

On top of the pre-baked butter dough bases in the rings, place a fine 2 mm layer of ground almond broyage (50% ground almost, 50% caster sugar), and add on top some sour cherries (de-stoned griottes).
Then pour the clafoutis filling into the moulds (about 3 cm high).
Bake for about 18 minutes at 170°C. Remove the baking rings once the clafoutis is sufficiently cool and stiff.

WHITE CHOCOLATE CRÈME (BEATABLE GANACHE)

Ingredients
160 g cream (35%)
½ vanilla stick
240 g white chocolate
12 g gelatine (or 1 gelatine leaf)
350 g cream (35%)

Preparation
Make a ganache of the smallest amount of cream, the scraped-out vanilla stick and the white chocolate. For this, heat the cream to 60°C, add the soaked gelatine and mix through a fine sieve into the molten white chocolate.
Wait until all the chocolate is absorbed in the mass and then mix into an emulsion (ganache). Then add the remainder of the liquid cream radially (3°C) and mix/emulsify again.
Chill for at least 6 hours at 3°C.
Beat this with the mixer at medium speed to the desired firmness (smoothly pipeable).

/// CONSTRUCTION ///

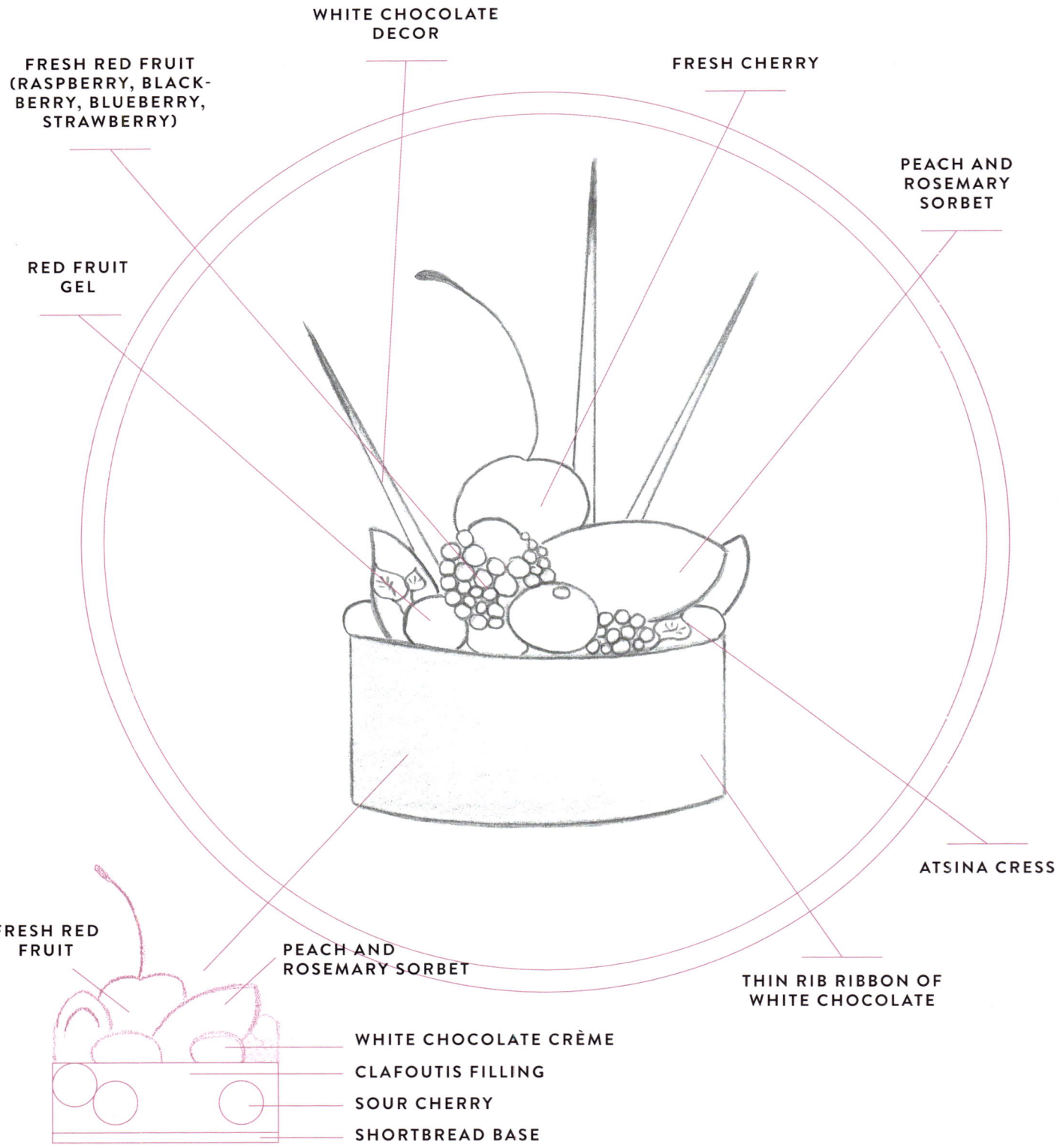

- WHITE CHOCOLATE DECOR
- FRESH CHERRY
- FRESH RED FRUIT (RASPBERRY, BLACKBERRY, BLUEBERRY, STRAWBERRY)
- PEACH AND ROSEMARY SORBET
- RED FRUIT GEL
- ATSINA CRESS
- FRESH RED FRUIT
- PEACH AND ROSEMARY SORBET
- THIN RIB RIBBON OF WHITE CHOCOLATE
- WHITE CHOCOLATE CRÈME
- CLAFOUTIS FILLING
- SOUR CHERRY
- SHORTBREAD BASE

PEACH AND ROSEMARY SORBET

Ingredients
225 g water
180 g caster sugar
40 g glucose powder
combined stabilizer (emulsifier and stabilizer)
4 sprigs of fresh rosemary, about 20 cm long
500 g peach pulp, with 10% sugar

Preparation
Mix the dry ingredients (caster sugar, glucose powder and combined stabilizer), add to the warm water and heat further to 70°C.
Cover with cling film and infuse the fresh rosemary in the syrup for about fifteen minutes.
Lastly pour this through a fine sieve onto the peach pulp (3°C) and mix well.
Pour the sorbet at 3° into the ice churn and churn the sorbet. Then immediately fill the 3D quenelles and freeze.

RED FRUIT GEL

Ingredients
85 g strawberries
85 g raspberry purée with 10% sugar
85 g cherry purée with 10% sugar
50 g sugar water 1/1
2 g agar agar

Preparation
Mix the fresh strawberries with the fruit purées, pass through a fine sieve and bring slowly to the boil with the sugar water and the agar agar.
Pour immediately through a fine sieve and store at 3°C. Before using, mix to a smooth gel.

COMPOSITION AND PRESENTATION OF THE DESSERT

Place round the chilled clafoutis a thin rib ribbon of white chocolate (4 cm high, 1 cm higher than the clafoutis) brushed in advance with a mixture of cocoa butter and red powder colouring (chocolate technique p. 30).
Fill further with a mixture of red fruit and a few cups of white chocolate cream and the gel of red fruits.
Finish with a quenelle of peach-rosemary sorbet and some white chocolate spears.

CRISPY BISCUIT

Ingredients
125 g butter
2 g vanilla essence
125 g icing sugar
125 g egg white
150 g flour
2 g salt

Preparation
Cream the butter and vanilla into a soft, smooth crème and mix in the icing sugar. Blend in the egg whites (at room temperature), followed by the sieved flour and salt.
Spread out the resulting mass onto a Silpat baking mat with a pre-cut template (rectangle) and bake golden brown at 200°C. After baking, remove immediately from the baking tray and fold around the clafoutis (or previously around a baking mould of the same diameter).
When presenting a lukewarm clafoutis, only the red fruit with the red-fruit gel is used as finishing.

BART'S TIPS

Prefer lukewarm clafoutis? This is perfectly doable! Replace the chocolate ribbon with a ribbon of crispy biscuit.

Tangerine – passion fruit fruity bitter chocolate

A strong but fruity chocolate. It's not only the sour passion fruit flavours but also the predominant tangerine tastes in particular that give the fresh balance. The croquant of white caramelized chocolate is a very nice addition.

FRUITY BITTER CHOCOLATE CRÈME

Ingredients
180 g whole milk
20 g sushi vinegar
50 g egg yolks
60 g caster sugar
12 g gelatine (or 1 gelatine leaf)
120 g bitter chocolate 64%
   (with fresh-sour fruity touch)
80 g fondant chocolate

Preparation
Prepare an anglaise (83°C) with the first four ingredients. Remove from the heat and add the soaked gelatine. Pour the mixture through a fine sieve onto the two chocolates. Emulsify to an emulsion (ganache).
Place a 4 mm layer of bitter chocolate crème in a Silpat baking mat (ring).

CRÈME OF CARAMELIZED WHITE CHOCOLATE

Pre-preparation
Vacuum the desired amount of white chocolate and cook in a hot water bath at 85°C for 8 hours. This will caramelize the sugars present in the white chocolate.

Ingredients
200 g whole milk
50 g egg yolks
60 g caster sugar
30 g gelatine (or 2½ gelatine leaves)
200 g white chocolate, caramelized
pinch of salt

Preparation
Prepare an anglaise (83°C) with the first three ingredients. Remove from the heat and add the soaked gelatine. Then pour the mass through a fine sieve onto the chopped caramelized chocolate and salt. Emulsify (mix) to a homogeneous mass. Leave to crystallize completely in the refrigerator to form a sprayable crème.

PASSION FRUIT CRÉMEUX

Ingredients
250 g passionfruit juice with
   10% sugar
120 g egg yolks
70 g caster sugar
24 g gelatine (or gelatine 2 leaves)
85 g butter

Preparation
Prepare an anglaise (83°C) with the first three ingredients. Remove from the heat and add the soaked gelatine. Pour through a fine sieve and mix in the soft butter at 38°C to produce an emulsion/homogeneous mass.
Place the passion fruit crémeux into a 3D quenelle silicone mat and freeze for further use.
Glaze afterwards with a neutral jelly with some 15-20% passion purée added. Heat this glaze to 50°C to ensure a thin layer of jelly around the crémeux.

BART'S TIPS

To finish, spray the thin ring of fruity bitter chocolate cream (base) with a yellow chocolate spray (50% white chocolate, 50% cocoa butter and a little fat-soluble yellow colouring). This gives a more stylish result.

/// CONSTRUCTION ///

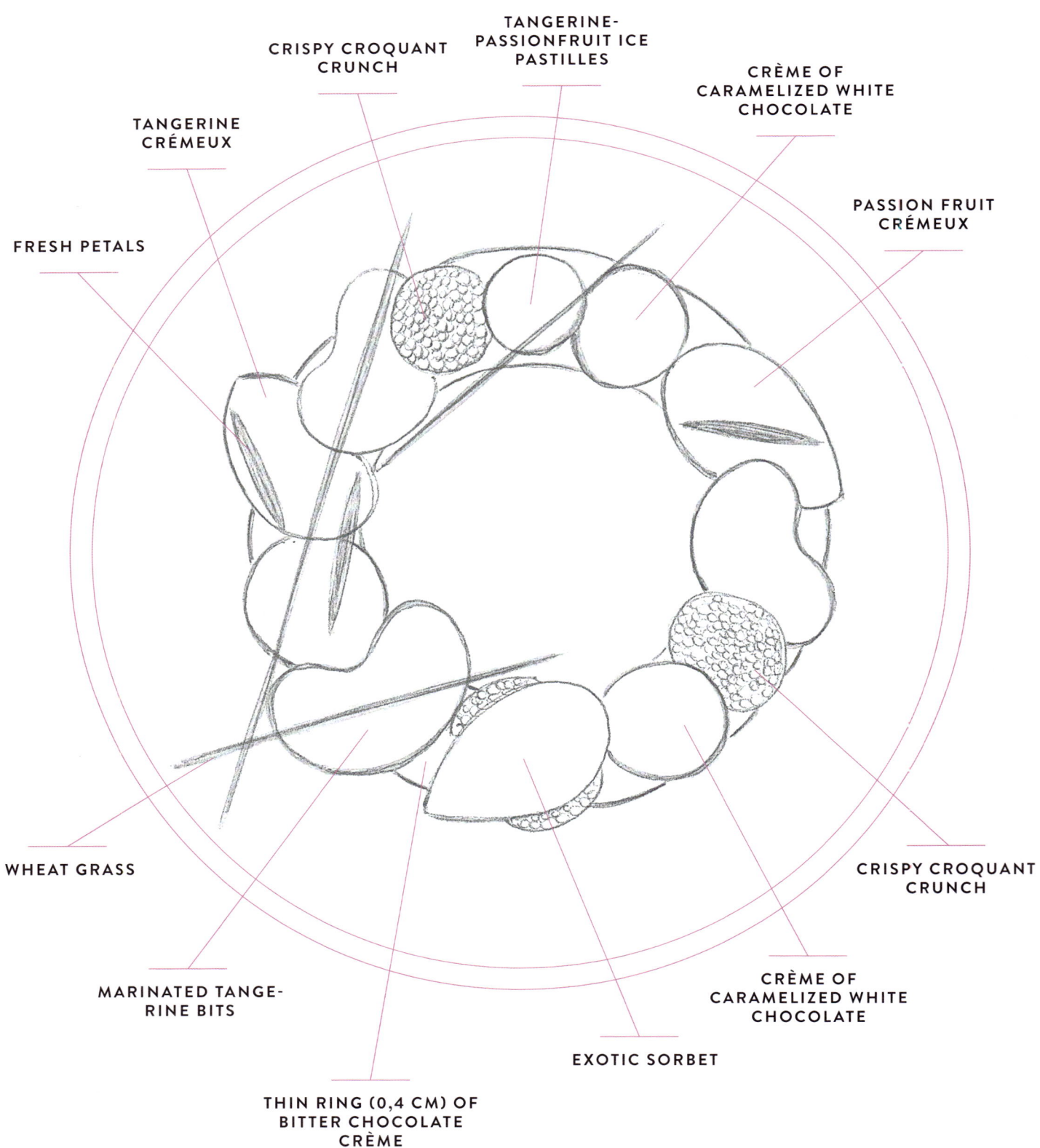

- CRISPY CROQUANT CRUNCH
- TANGERINE-PASSIONFRUIT ICE PASTILLES
- CRÈME OF CARAMELIZED WHITE CHOCOLATE
- TANGERINE CRÉMEUX
- PASSION FRUIT CRÉMEUX
- FRESH PETALS
- WHEAT GRASS
- CRISPY CROQUANT CRUNCH
- MARINATED TANGERINE BITS
- CRÈME OF CARAMELIZED WHITE CHOCOLATE
- EXOTIC SORBET
- THIN RING (0,4 CM) OF BITTER CHOCOLATE CRÈME

TANGERINE CRÉMEUX

Ingredients

250 g tangerine juice, with
   10% sugar
120 g egg yolks
60 g caster sugar
24 g gelatine (or 2 gelatine leaves)
85 g butter

Preparation

Prepare an anglaise (83°C) with the first four ingredients. Remove from the heat and add the soaked gelatine. Pour through a fine sieve and mix in the soft butter at 38°C to produce an emulsion/homogeneous mass.
Place the tangerine crémeux into a 3D quenelle silicone mat.
Glaze afterwards with a neutral jelly with some 15-20% tangerine purée added. Heat this glaze to 50°C to ensure a thin layer of jelly around the crémeux.

MARINATED TANGERINE BITS

Ingredients

3 peeled tangerines
250 g tangerine juice, with
   10% sugar
50 g sugar water (1/1)
25 g orange liqueur

Preparation

Peel and remove the pith from the tangerines. Place the desired quantity of tangerine bits in a vacuum bag together with the coulis of tangerine juice, sugar water and orange juice. Create a 65% vacuum and leave overnight in the refrigerator.

EXOTIC SORBET

Ingredients

260 g water
150 g caster sugar
80 g atomized glucose
combined stabilizer (emulsifier
   and stablizer)
300 g mango purée with 10% sugar
90 g passion fruit purée with
   10% sugar
60 g lime juice
40 g banana

Preparation

Heat the water to around 40°C and add to the mixture of caster sugar, atomized glucose and stabilizer. Wait half an hour until the sugars are optimally dissolved and the stabilizer is lightly bonded. Then mix with the fruit juices. Check with a refractometer that the mixture is at 30°Brix (see also p. 20) and churn. Place immediately into a 3D silicone quenelle mat and freeze for use.

CRISPY CROQUANT CRUNCH

Mix rice crispies with a quantity of pre-crystallized white chocolate and possibly a little neutral oil (grape seed oil). Roll out immediately between two sheets of baking paper and press out the desired shapes or leave to crystallize and cut with a cutter into crunch.

TANGERINE-PASSIONFRUIT ICE PASTILLES

Ingredients

300 g tangerine purée with
   10% sugar
100 g passion fruit purée with
   10% sugar
30 g caster sugar
0.5 g xanthan gum (cold binder)

Preparation

Boil the fruit purées together and reduce to 300 g. Fold in the mixture of caster sugar and cold binder and place the mixture in a small 3D ball mat (1 cm diameter balls). Freeze for further use. Decorate last.

FINISHING

Finish with a few tufts of wheat grass and fresh petals.

Beetroot – chocolate – raspberry

Beetroot and chocolate? It's a real challenge to soften the sharp taste of beetroot with the chocolate and fruity character of raspberries without losing the earthiness of the beetroot. A good food pairing translates into an attractive balance between the beetroot, soft chocolate and fresh-sour raspberry flavour.

MILK CHOCOLATE (40%) MOUSSE WITH RASPBERRIES

Ingredients
175 g raspberry purée with 10% sugar
36 g gelatine (or 3 gelatine leaves)
250 g milk chocolate (40%)
50 g cooking foam
250 g cream (35%)

Preparation
Heat the raspberry purée to 40°C in order to easily mix the gelatine. Add the milk chocolate (40°C) and mix the whole to a homogeneous mass (emulsion).
Fold in the cooking foam lightly at 35°C.
Mix the 2/3 whipped cream into the whole.

BEETROOT MOUSSE

Ingredients
24 g gelatine (or 2 gelatine leaves)
80 g cooking foam
150 g beetroot purée
125 g cream (35%)

Preparation
Mix the soaked and melted gelatine into the lukewarm cooking foam. Then distribute and mix in the beetroot purée, both into the lukewarm cooking foam and the 2/3 whipped cream.
Lastly fold the beetroot-cooking foam mixture in two goes into the beetroot-cream mass to produce a smooth, airy mousse.

ITALIAN FOAM (COOKING FOAM)

Ingredients
80 g water
300 g caster sugar
200 g egg white
30 g caster sugar

Preparation
Bring the water and most of the caster sugar gently to the boil.
Meanwhile, beat the egg whites with the rest of the caster sugar at medium speed.
Boil the sugar water to 121°C. Then add in a uniform jet to the stiffly, but smoothly beaten egg whites.
Beat this 'Italian foam' at medium speed until cold.

BEETROOT JELLY

Ingredients
200 g beetroot purée
24 g gelatine (or 2 gelatine leaves)

Preparation
Heat the beetroot purée to 40°C and dissolve the soaked gelatine into it.
Pour into a mould of your choice and, once sufficiently gelled, cut into cubes of the desired size.

SUGAR AND BEETROOT GLAZE

Ingredients
10 g beetroot powder
125 g caster sugar
150 g natural beet juice
175 g glucose
150 g white chocolate
100 g sweetened condensed milk
78 g gelatine (or 6½ gelatine leaves)

Preparation
Mix the beetroot powder with the caster sugar and bring to the boil with the beetroot juice and glucose.
Then pour the mixture onto the white chocolate and the soaked gelatine.
Lastly stir in the sweetened condensed

/// CONSTRUCTION ///

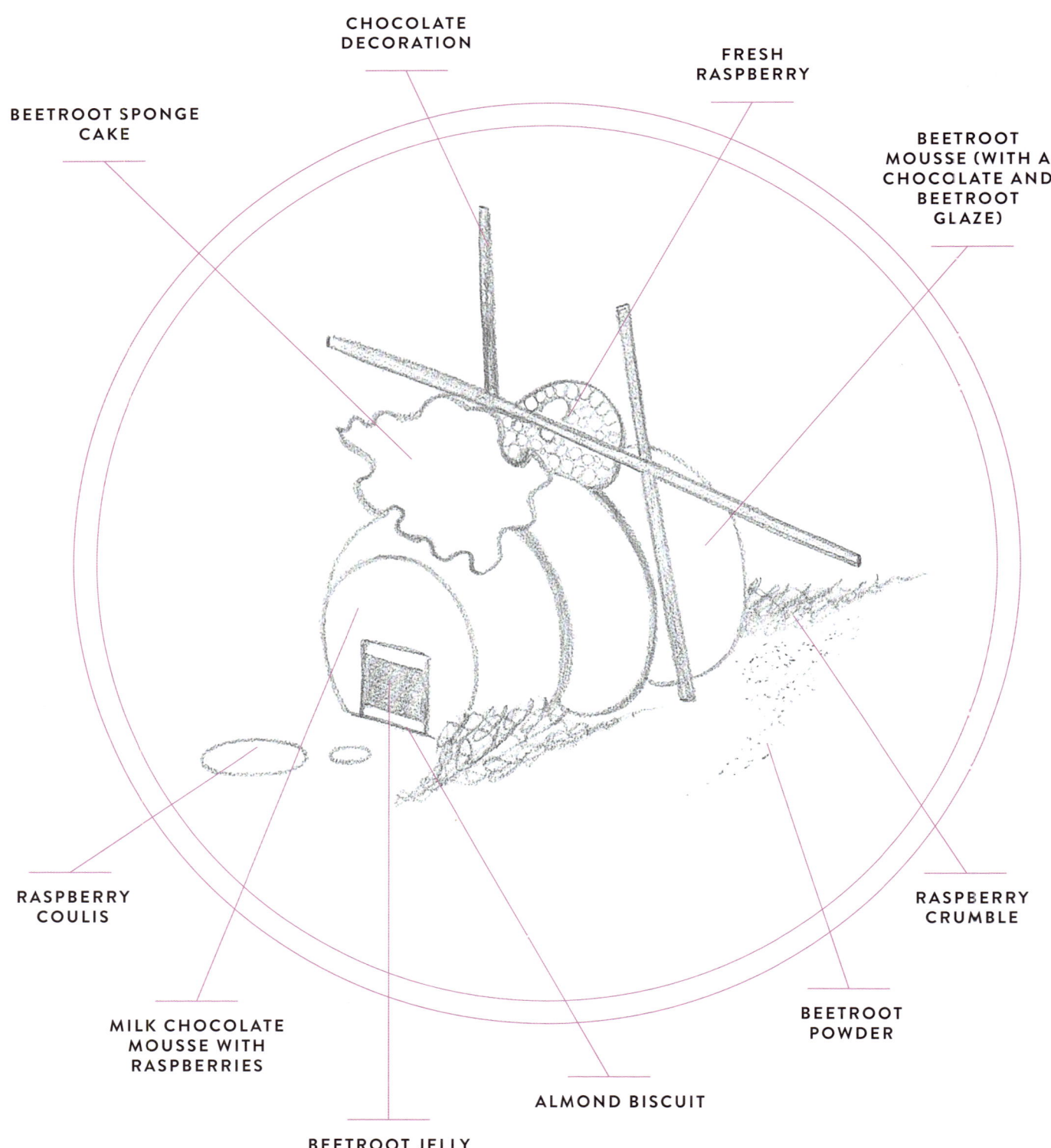

- BEETROOT SPONGE CAKE
- CHOCOLATE DECORATION
- FRESH RASPBERRY
- BEETROOT MOUSSE (WITH A CHOCOLATE AND BEETROOT GLAZE)
- RASPBERRY COULIS
- MILK CHOCOLATE MOUSSE WITH RASPBERRIES
- BEETROOT JELLY
- ALMOND BISCUIT
- BEETROOT POWDER
- RASPBERRY CRUMBLE

milk and mix the whole into an emulsion (homogeneous mass).
Cover and leave to chill in the refrigerator (3°C) until completely crystallized. Before glazing, reheat the mix to 35°C to pour over/glaze the pre-chilled pastries (-20°C).

BEETROOT SPONGE CAKE

Ingredients
150 g pasteurized egg white
40 g grape seed oil
35 g beetroot powder
0.25 g red powder colouring
20 g icing sugar
45 g flour
1 g salt

Preparation
In the Thermomix, mix the egg white and oil with the sieved mixture of beetroot powder, powder colouring, icing sugar, flour and salt. Fill the siphon bottle with the finely mixed mass.
Then add some gas cartridges (N2O) and mix the gas into the mixture by shaking the siphon bottle hard (good gas distribution).
Fill the isomo (insulating foam) cups half-full with the frothy mass and bake for about twenty seconds in a powerful microwave oven. After baking, turn the cups upside down immediately onto baking paper to avoid drying out.

RASPBERRY CRUMBLE

Ingredients
125 g butter
125 g caster sugar
50 g raspberry powder
150 g flour

Preparation
Chop the butter (at room temperature) into blocks and, using the mixer (spatula), fold in the caster sugar and raspberry powder. Lastly, fold in the sifted flour.
Crumble the crumble onto a Silpat and dry in the oven at 90°C.
During baking/drying, mix the crumble regularly for a smooth baking. In this way, you preserve the natural colour of the raspberry powder.

ALMOND BISCUIT
See p. 134

FINISHING
A few drops of beetroot juice
A little beetroot powder
Chocolate decoration: for the technique, see QR code p. 61
Thin chocolate stripes

BART'S TIPS

Bake the raspberry crumble at a lower temperature than normal; this will retain the light red colour of the crumble. For a fresher, red raspberry colour, mix with a little raspberry powder after baking.

Golden chocolate bar

Not a dessert for softies: chocoholics will be attracted by the sophisticated selection of cocoa beans that translate into a soft crème, combined with a rich almond-chocolate biscuit and a great caramel- hazelnut crunch!

CHOCOLATE-ALMOND BISCUIT

Ingredients
180 g egg yolks
135 g almond broyage (50% ground almonds + 50% caster sugar)
65 g caster sugar
170 g egg white
70 g caster sugar
60 g flour
40 g cocoa powder
60 g butter

Result: 780 g, for two 30 × 40 cm baking plates.

Preparation
Beat the first three ingredients together with the beater to a fluffy mixture.
Beat the egg whites firmly but smoothly and fold in with the caster sugar into the fluffy mixture of egg yolk, ground almond and caster sugar.
Gradually add the sieved flour-cocoa powder mixture. Last of all, fold in the melted butter (40°C).
Spread evenly on baking paper or a baking mat and bake at 230°C for about six minutes.
Immediately after baking remove the biscuit from the baking tray to avoid further drying.

HAZELNUT-CARAMEL CRUNCH

Ingredients
3 g pectin
150 g caster sugar
10 g water
50 g glucose
80 g butter
60 g hazelnuts
1 g coarse sea salt

Preparation
Mix the pectin with the caster sugar and bring to the boil together with the water, glucose and butter. Then add the lightly roasted and coarsely broken hazelnuts and the sea salt.
Pour the mix immediately onto a Silpat baking mat, spread evenly and leave to cool completely.
Bake at 160°C until a uniform golden brown caramel is formed. For this, stir the mass regularly.
Break or cut the caramel after complete cooling to the desired crunch.

ORIGIN CHOCOLATE CRÈME

Ingredients
200 g whole milk
105 g cream
70 g egg yolks
30 g invert sugar
215 g origin chocolate 64%
210 g fondant chocolate
440 g cream (35%)

Preparation
Prepare an anglaise (83°C) of the first four ingredients and then add to the two chocolates through a fine sieve. Mix the whole into a smooth emulsion once both chocolates have been absorbed into the mass.
At 28-30°C, mix the 2/3 whipped cream to produce a thick but smooth and sprayable structure.

/// CONSTRUCTION ///

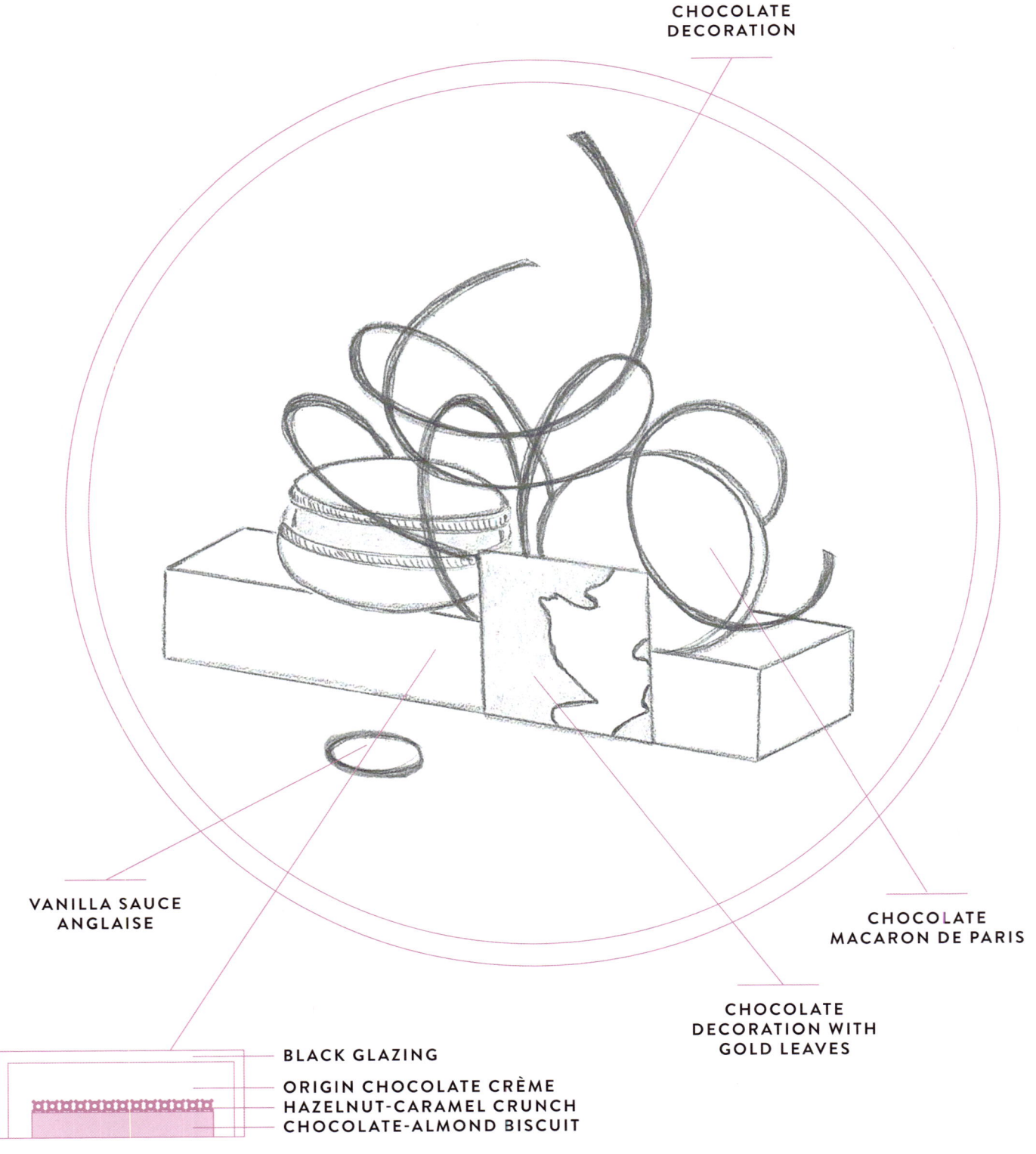

CHOCOLATE DECORATION

CHOCOLATE MACARON DE PARIS

CHOCOLATE DECORATION WITH GOLD LEAVES

VANILLA SAUCE ANGLAISE

BLACK GLAZING
ORIGIN CHOCOLATE CRÈME
HAZELNUT-CARAMEL CRUNCH
CHOCOLATE-ALMOND BISCUIT

BLACK GLAZING

Ingredients
110 g water
50 g glucose
110 g dextrose
110 g cream (35%)
350 g caster sugar
140 g cocoa powder
240 g neutral jelly
156 g gelatine (or 13 gelatine leaves)

Preparation
Heat the first five ingredients to 50°C and add to the sieved cocoa powder. Bring to the boil and add through a fine sieve to the neutral jelly and the soaked gelatine.
Mix the glaze without adding air and leave to crystallize fully before use (3°C).
Before glazing, reheat the mix to 35°C to pour over/glaze the pre-chilled pastries (-20°C).

CHOCOLATE MACARON DE PARIS

Ingredients
200 g egg white
230 g caster sugar
190 g icing sugar
25 g cocoa powder
215 g very fine almond powder

Preparation
Sieve the icing sugar with the cocoa powder and almond powder. Beat the egg white firm but smooth with the caster sugar (add the sugar gradually). Mix the icing sugar, cocoa powder and almond powder together and add gradually to the smoothly whipped egg white and mix to the desired pipeable consistency.
Using an icing bag, pipe evenly-sized (2.5 cm diameter) macaroons (macaroon shells) onto silicone mats. Leave to crust for about 30 minutes before placing in the oven.
Bake at 150°C for about 14 minutes.

GANACHE (MACAROON FILLING)

Ingredients
300 g cream (35%)
200 g fondant chocolate 60%
150 g milk chocolate

Preparation
Heat the cream (45°C) and add gradually to the mixture of melted fondant chocolate and milk chocolate (45°C). Mix the whole (emulsify) into a smooth homogeneous mass (emulsion).
Leave to crystallize.
Cool for further use.

COMPOSITION AND FINISHING OF THE MACAROONS
Fill the macaroon shells with the soft ganache. Place in the refrigerator to firm.

VANILLA SAUCE ANGLAISE

Ingredients
200 g whole milk
300 g cream (35%)
1 vanilla stick
240 g egg yolks
130 g caster sugar

Preparation
Heat the whole milk with the cream and scrapped-out vanilla stick to 90°C and leave to infuse (15 minutes, covered, for optimal taste development).
Remove the vanilla stick. Pour the infusion through a fine sieve onto the mixture of egg yolks and caster sugar.
Make an anglaise by heating and stirring to 83°C. Pour immediately through a fine sieve into a bowl. Cover and leave to cool completely to 3°C.
In use, this structure is 'thickly liquid', that is, the anglaise does not run out.

FINISHING
Gold leaves, gold glitter

Lime – lemon

A very fresh-tart dessert of mainly lime and lemon!
The overall composition includes a lime-lemon crémeux on top of lightly candied lime chunks in a citrus syrup and lemongrass-mint gelee, with a vanilla sponge cake and a soft meringue as a sweet counterpart.

LEMON-LIME CRÉMEUX

Ingredients
125 g fresh lemon juice
125 g fresh lime juice
grated zest of 1 lime
150 g caster sugar
160 g eggs
140 g egg yolks
30 g gelatine (or 2½ gelatine leaves)
150 g butter

Preparation
Make an anglaise by heating and stirring the first six ingredients to 83°C, and then adding the soaked gelatine. At 38°C, add the softened butter and mix everything homogeneously to a smooth emulsion (crémeux).
Place the crémeux into a 3D silicone ball mat and freeze for further use. Remove from the mould. Glaze the resulting lemon-lime crémeux with a neutral jelly to which 5% lime juice (or lime zest) and a few drops of yellow liquid colouring have been added.
Heat the glaze to 50°C to obtain optimal and thin adhesion around the crémeux.

LIGHTLY CANDIED LIME CHUNKS

Ingredients
500 g water
750 g caster sugar
2 stalks of lemongrass
juice of 1 lime
grated zest of 2 limes
2 bunches mint
75 g white rum

Preparation
Bring the water to the boil with the caster sugar, remove from the heat and add the chopped lemon grass stems, lime juice, lime zest and bunches of mint. Cover and leave to infuse for half an hour. This allows the flavour to develop optimally in the syrup.
Pour the infusion through a conical sieve (not a fine sieve, which will block the lime zest) and add slices of lime 'peeled alive' (the skin and pith are removed with a knife and the chunks of flesh cut out from between the membranes). Add the white rum to the cooled mixture. Then the lime particles are vacuum-infused.

WHAT IS VACUUM INFUSION?
This is a technique whereby the cell walls/pores of the lime particles are swollen and even broken open by the high pressure in the vacuum device. This enables the fruit to be much more easily saturated with the liquid present, without damaging the fruit.
Keeping ingredients in a vacuum bag is not only convenient, but being fully sealed off from air, they keep longer.

LIGHTLY BOUND LEMON GRASS-MINT JELLY

Ingredients
250 g infused syrup of lemon grass, lime (from the lime chunks) and mint
36 g gelatine (or 3 gelatine leaves)

Preparation
Add the still warm infused syrup to the soaked gelatine and pour in a 3mm thick layer onto a Silpat baking mat. Freeze and then press out the desired diameters.

/// CONSTRUCTION ///

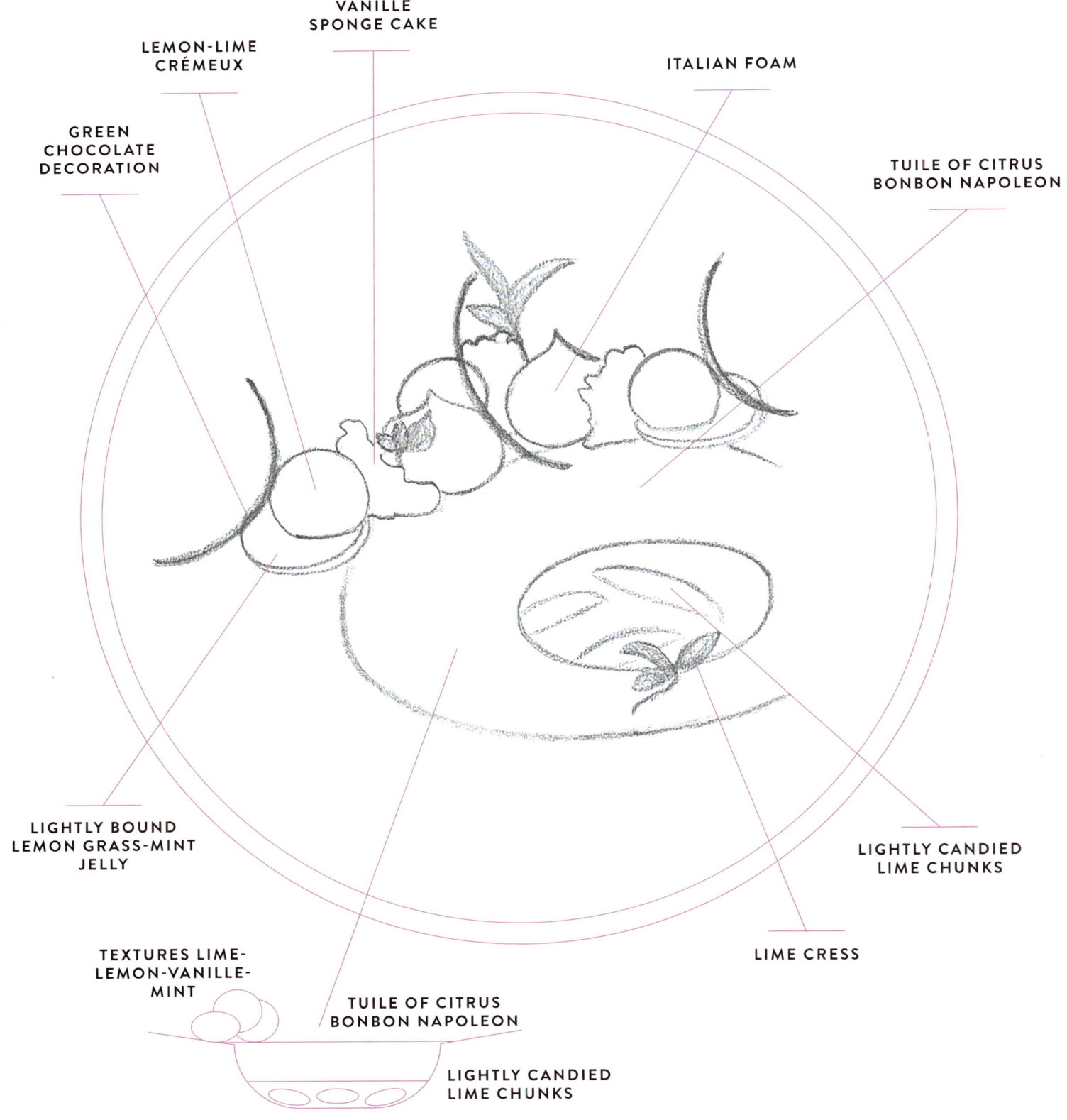

VANILLE SPONGE CAKE

Ingredients

125 g almond powder
125 g icing sugar
25 g flour
2 g vanilla powder (100% vanilla stick)
165 g egg white
100 g egg yolks
15 g grape seed oil

Preparation

Mix all the dry ingredients (almond powder, icing sugar, flour and vanilla powder) sufficiently finely with each other. Only then add the egg white, egg yolks and oil and mix for another sixty seconds at Thermomix setting 5.
Rub the mass through a fine sieve before placing in a spray siphon. Then add some gas cartridges (N2O) and mix the gas into the mixture by shaking the siphon bottle hard (good gas distribution).
Fill the isomo (insulating foam) cups half-full with the frothy mass and bake for about twenty seconds in a powerful microwave oven. After baking, turn the cups upside down immediately onto baking paper to avoid drying out.

ITALIAN FOAM (COOKING FOAM)

Ingredients

80 g water
300 g caster sugar
200 g egg white
30 g caster sugar

Preparation

Bring the water and most of the caster sugar gently to the boil.
Meanwhile, beat the egg whites with the rest of the caster sugar at medium speed. Boil the sugar water to 121°C. Then add in a uniform jet to the stiffly, but smoothly beaten egg whites.
Beat this 'Italian foam' at medium speed until cold.
Using an icing bag and a smooth nozzle, place attractive drops with pointed tips onto the plate.

TUILE OF CITRUS BONBON NAPOLEON

Mix citrus bonbon Napoleons (boiled sweets with soft sugar centre) to powder in the Thermomix and sprinkle the resulting powder through a fine sieve and a template onto a silicone mat. Bake briefly at 150°C (only melting, not discolouring) and allow to cool completely before removing for further use.

FINISHING

Green chocolate decoration (for chocolate techniques, see p. 29)
Grated lime zest
Lime cress

BART'S TIPS

Using the remains of the syrup of lightly candied citrus particles, it is easy to make a delicious, transparent jelly with lots of flavour (lightly-bound lemongrass-mint gelée). Take care that the sugar decoration on the sweets only melts in the oven and does not caramelize.

Chocolate – chestnut – calamansi

A surprising dessert with chocolate and chestnut in the main role, combined with the fresh acids of the calamansi, giving a full range of flavours from unctuous macaroon and chocolate to fresh chestnut (sorbet) to the acid touch of the calamansi.

MACAROONS

Ingredients
200 g icing sugar
200 g almond powder (100%)
80 g egg white
50 g water
190 g caster sugar
75 g egg white
10 g caster sugar

Preparation
Sift the icing sugar with the very fine almond powder and mix this with the 80 g of egg white at room temperature.
Boil the water with the sugar to 118°C and add it in a jet to the 75 g egg white, beaten firm but smooth with the small amount of sugar (caster sugar).
When the cooking foam has cooled to about 50°C, it is folded in, in two goes, into the smooth mass of egg white, almond powder and icing sugar.
Mix everything even more homogeneously until the desired firmness/piping consistency of the macaroon batter is obtained.
Using an icing bag, pipe even-sized macaroons (2.5 cm diameter) onto silicone mats and sprinkle with feuilletine before baking. Leave to crust for about 30 minutes before placing in the oven.
Bake at 150°C for about 14 minutes.

GANACHE (MACAROON FILLING)

Ingredients
300 g cream (35%)
200 g fondant chocolate 60%
150 g milk chocolate

Preparation
Heat the cream to 45°C and add gradually to the mixture of melted fondant chocolate and milk chocolate (45°C). Mix the whole and emulsify into a smooth homogeneous emulsion. Leave to crystallize.
Cool to desired piping consistency for further use.

COMPOSITION AND FINISHING OF THE MACAROONS
Fill the macaroon shells with the soft ganache, leave in the refrigerator to firm sufficiently and sprinkle finally with a mixture of alcohol (98%) and silver powder.

3D CHOCOLATE/CALAMANSI BALLS

1. CHOCOLATE FLAN
Ingredients
250 g whole milk
50 g cream (35%)
40 g caster sugar
15 g cornflour
45 g egg yolks
200 g fondant chocolate
pinch of fleur de sel

Preparation
Make an anglaise by heating and stirring the first five ingredients to 83°C. Add this through a sieve to the chocolate and salt. Mix the mass once the chocolate is completely melted. Emulsify to a smooth emulsion.
Place the chocolate flan into Silpat baking mats (small 3D ball – 10g) but only half fill the moulds. Cool before using further.

/// CONSTRUCTION ///

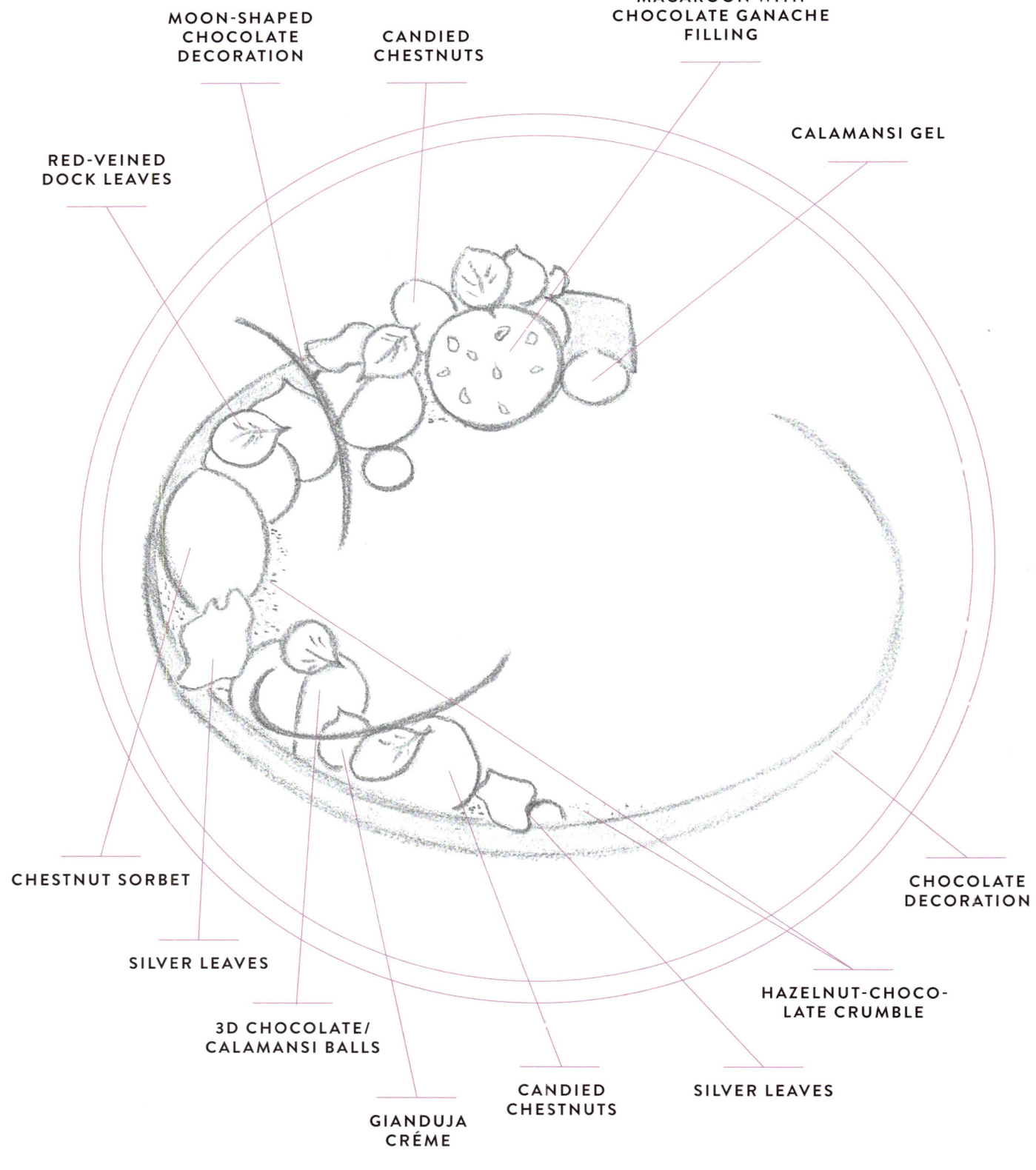

- MOON-SHAPED CHOCOLATE DECORATION
- CANDIED CHESTNUTS
- MACAROON WITH CHOCOLATE GANACHE FILLING
- CALAMANSI GEL
- RED-VEINED DOCK LEAVES
- CHESTNUT SORBET
- CHOCOLATE DECORATION
- SILVER LEAVES
- HAZELNUT-CHOCOLATE CRUMBLE
- 3D CHOCOLATE/CALAMANSI BALLS
- CANDIED CHESTNUTS
- SILVER LEAVES
- GIANDUJA CRÉME

2. CALAMANSI CRÉMEUX

Ingredients
185 g calamansi juice
35 g water
175 g caster sugar
150 g eggs
36 g gelatine (or 3 gelatine leaves)
200 g butter

Preparation
Prepare an anglaise (83°C) with the calamansi juice, water, caster sugar and eggs. Add through a sieve to the soaked gelatine. Leave to cool to 40°C and only then add the soft butter. Mix the mass homogeneously to an emulsion.
Fill the 3D moulds (small 3D balls – 10 g) which are already half filled with the chocolate flan with the calamansi crémeux.

CHESTNUT SORBET

Ingredients
390 g water
175 g caster sugar
25 g glucose powder
combined stabilizer (emulsifier and stabilizer)
600 g chestnut purée
7 g whisky (40°)

Preparation
Mix the dry ingredients (caster sugar, atomized glucose and combined stabilizer) and then add to the water at about 50°C. Once the sugars are fully dissolved, add the chestnut purée with the whisky. Churn the yoghurt sorbet and place immediately into 3D quenelle moulds. Freeze.

GIANDUJA CRÉME

Ingredients
200 g whole milk
60 g egg yolks
10 g caster sugar
24 g gelatine (or 2 gelatine leaves)
35 g milk chocolate (40%)
265 g gianduja hazelnut

Preparation
Prepare an anglaise (83°C) of whole milk, egg yolks and caster sugar. Pass through a fine sieve immediately and pour, in three rounds, into the chopped milk chocolate and gianduja mixture. Mix the whole into an emulsion and cool before use (3°C).
Stir the crémeux smooth and apply pretty 'tops' with a smooth spray nozzle.

HAZELNUT-CHOCOLATE CRUMBLE

Ingredients
150 g roasted hazelnuts
150 g bitter, fruity origin chocolate 70%

Preparation
Roast the peeled hazelnuts at 150° C to a uniform caramel colour and allow to cool completely.
Chop or cut the chocolate and the nuts separately into a fine grain size and mix.

CALAMANSI GEL

Ingredients
125 g caster sugar
1 g gellan gum
7 g agar agar
330 g calamansi juice
170 g water

Preparation

Mix the caster sugar with the gellan gum and the agar agar. Add to the mixture of calamansi juice and water.

Then bring all ingredients to the boil in order to bind.

Pour the mixture through a fine sieve into a plastic basin. Cover and leave to cool and gel fully.

Just before using, mix smooth with the Thermomix, eventually rubbing through a very fine sieve until the desired gel structure is reached.

FURTHER DECORATION

Red-veined dock leaves ('cress')
Candied chestnuts
Calamansi gel
Red-black chocolate curls (see chocolate decorations on p. 32)
Moon-shaped chocolate decoration (see chocolate decorations on p. 29)
Silver leaves

Orange – bergamot – basil

A southern dessert with flavours like orange combined with bergamot from northern Italy and an accent of fresh basil. The chocolate crumble with southern influences makes for a great crunch between the various tastes.

ORANGE CRÉMEUX

Ingredients
235 g fresh orange juice
15 g concentrated orange juice (frozen)
120 g egg yolks
60 g caster sugar
24 g gelatine (or 2 gelatine leaves)
85 g butter

Preparation
Prepare an anglaise (83°C) with the first four ingredients. Remove from the heat and add the soaked gelatine. Pour through a fine sieve and mix in the butter at 38-40°C to produce a homogeneous emulsion.
Place the orange crémeux into a 3D silicone mat and chill for further processing.

Remove the orange crémeux balls from the mould and glaze with a neutral jelly (50°C), flavoured and coloured with 10% fresh orange juice, eventually with a little concentrated orange juice and a few drops of yellow-orange liquid colouring.

BERGAMOT-BASIL CRÉMEUX

Ingredients
50 g of basil juice (see below)
105 g bergamot juice
190 g egg white
grated zest of 4 bergamots
150 g caster sugar
30 g gelatine (or 2½ gelatine leaves)
265 g butter

Preparation
First blanch the basil in hot water at 90°C and then place in ice water to keep the dark green colour. Next mix 50 g of blanched basil very finely with 100 g of cold water. This is the basil juice which forms the basis of the recipe.
Heat and stir the first five ingredients together to produce an anglaise (83°C) and then add to the soaked gelatine through a fine sieve. Allow to cool to 38°C before adding the soft butter to give a smooth emulsion (crémeux).
Place the bergamot-basil crémeux into the desired 3D silicone mat and chill in the deep-freeze.
Remove and glaze the crémeux with a neutral jelly (50°C), flavoured with a little basil juice, very lightly coloured with green liquid colouring.

ORANGE-HAZELNUT CRUMBLE BASE

Ingredients
145 g butter
220 g caster sugar
grated zest of 4 oranges
grated zest of 1 lemon
220 g fine-ground hazelnut powder
180 g flour
40 g cocoa powder
5 g coarse sea salt

Preparation
Mix the butter (at room temperature) with the caster sugar, citrus zest and the hazelnut powder. Then fold in the sieved mixture of flour, cocoa powder and coarse sea salt to produce a homogeneous butter dough.
Crumble the butter dough on a baking tray lined with baking paper and bake at 150°C for 20-25 minutes. During baking, mix the crumble to achieve an evenly baked result.

/// CONSTRUCTION ///

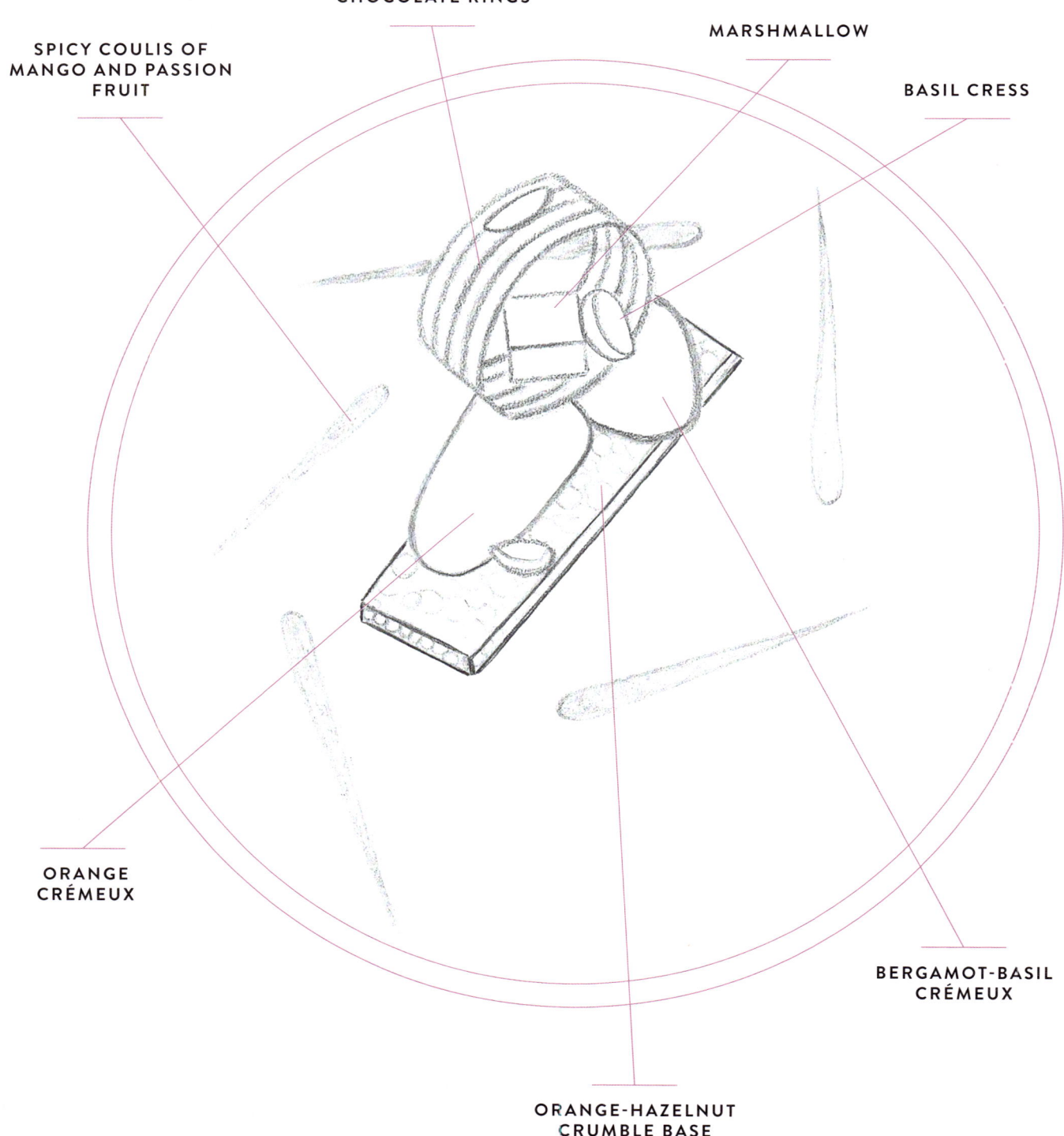

- FONDANT CHOCOLATE RINGS
- MARSHMALLOW
- BASIL CRESS
- SPICY COULIS OF MANGO AND PASSION FRUIT
- ORANGE CRÉMEUX
- BERGAMOT-BASIL CRÉMEUX
- ORANGE-HAZELNUT CRUMBLE BASE

COMPOSITION OF THE BASE

Ingredients
600 g crumble
60 g gianduja
120 g hazelnut paste 100%

Preparation
Stir the crumble – fully cooled and at the desired grain size – through a mixture of gianduja and hazelnut paste. Place the resulting crumble on a plate with the stainless steel mould of your choice and press down lightly.

SPICY COULIS OF MANGO AND PASSION FRUIT

Ingredients
15 g caster sugar
0.5 g xanthan gum (cold binder)
300 g spiced mango purée with 10% sugar
60 g passion fruit purée with 10% sugar
60 g invert sugar

Preparation
Mix the caster sugar with the xanthan gum and stir into the already mixed fruit purée and invert sugar.

FINISHING
Fondant chocolate rings (chocolate decoration p. 30)
Basil cress
Marshmallow (see p. 194)

Rhubarb – water melon – yoghurt – strawberry

*Rhubarb pairs surprisingly well with watermelon.
Rhubarb in different textures is the red thread running through the dessert, while the strawberries
and yoghurt, together with the crispy elements, make the dessert a lot more interesting.*

LIGHTLY COOKED RHUBARB STICKS

Ingredients
0,5 kg rhubarb
75 à 100 g caster sugar
1 brinch of fresh lemon verbena

Preparation
Cut the washed rhubarb, with its skin, into pieces of about 1 cm thick and place in a vacuum bag (85% vacuum) together with the necessary amount of caster sugar and fresh lemon verbena.
Cook in a 60°C hot water bath for thirty minutes (al dente).
Allow the cooked rhubarb to cool completely (3°C) in the vacuum bag before cutting open.

RHUBARB SORBET

Ingredients
225 g caster sugar
70 g atomized glucose
combined stabilizer (emulsifier and stabilizer)
250 g water
880 g fresh rhubarb juice (juice centrifuge)
a little lemon or lime juice

Preparation
Mix the dry ingredients (caster sugar, atomized glucose and combined stabilizer) with the warm water and heat further to 40°C. Leave for half an hour for optimal dissolving of the sugars and gelling of the stabilizer.
Only then add the rhubarb pulp (3°C) with the lemon-lime juice. Check the °Brix with a refractometer (these need to be between 29 and 31, see also page 20). Churn the rhubarb sorbet and place immediately into a 3D quenelle silicone mat. Freeze.

RHUBARB MERINGUE

Ingredients
80 g icing sugar
25 g albumin (dried egg-white powder)
200 g fresh rhubarb juice (juice centrifuge)

Preparation
Mix and sift the icing sugar and albumen.
Add to the rhubarb juice and beat at a medium speed setting into to a lightweight, pipeable mix.
Pipe even drops onto a silicone mat from the food drier and leave to dry for 6 hours at 65°C.

WHITE CHOCOLATE CRÈME (BEATABLE GANACHE)
See p. 127

YOGHURT CRUMBLE

Ingredients
190 g butter
190 g caster sugar
75 g yoghurt powder
220 g flour

Preparation
Mix the butter at room temperature with the caster sugar and yoghurt powder.
Fold in the sieved flour and mix to a homogeneous dough.
Bake at 150°C. During the baking process mix the crumble to produce an optimum and evenly baked golden-brown colour.
Leave to cool completely before cutting/mixing the crumble to the desired size.

/// CONSTRUCTION ///

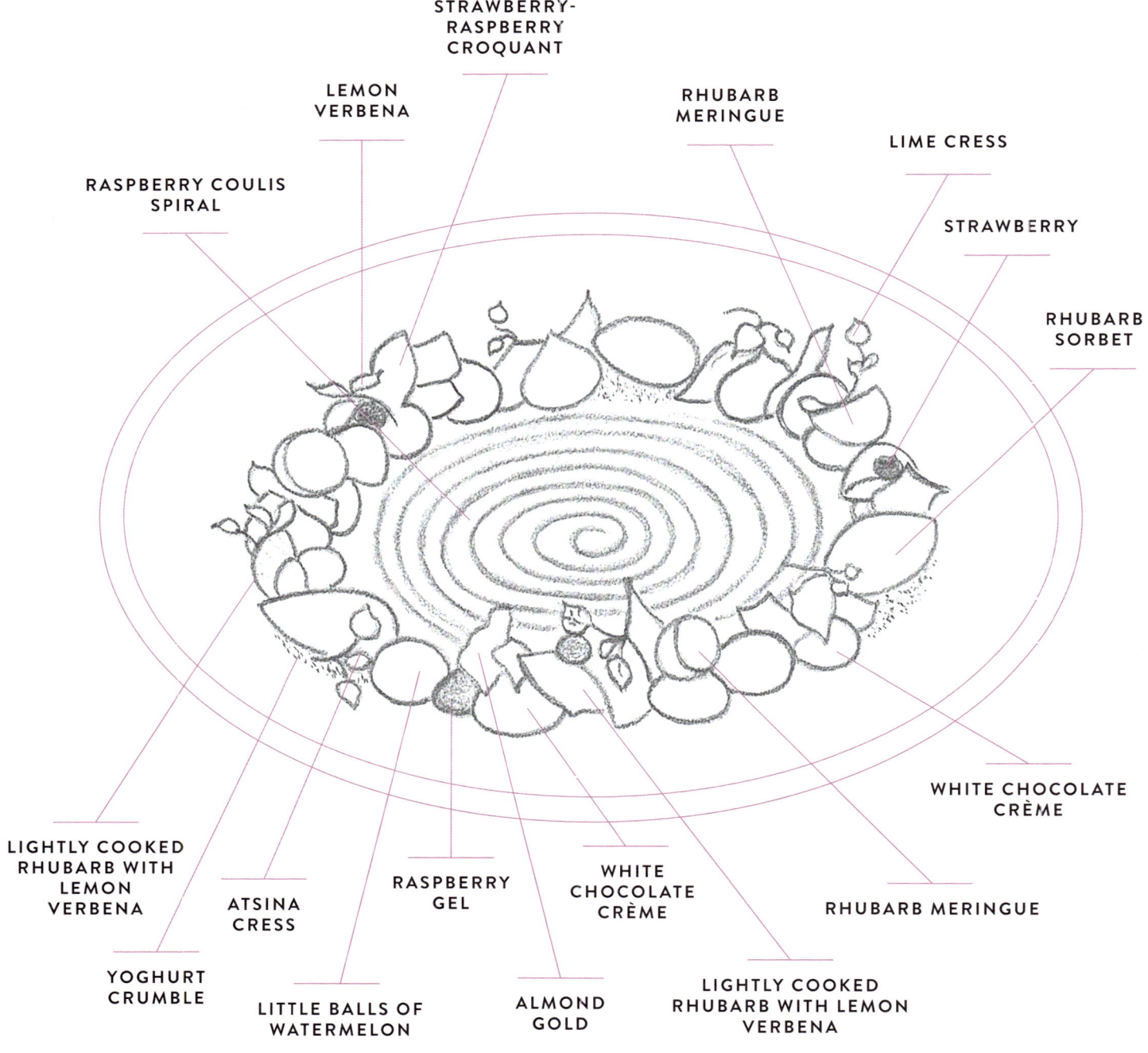

WHITE CHOCOLATE POWDER

Ingredients
50 g malto (Texturas)
100 g white chocolate

Preparation
Mix the malto with the molten white chocolate covering until an even powder is obtained. Keep fresh in an airtight container.

RASPBERRY COULIS

Ingredients
250 g raspberry purée with 10% sugar
30 g caster sugar

Preparation
Mix all ingredients.
Apply the coulis using the following technique: pour a quantity of raspberry coulis onto the plate and place it onto a gramophone turntable. As the plate spins, rub the raspberry coulis evenly with a brush.
Place the various flavours and textures around the coulis.

RASPBERRY GEL

Ingredients
250 g raspberry purée with 10% sugar
70 g sugar water 1/1
2.5 g agar agar

Preparation
Boil the raspberry purée with the sugar water and agar agar, pass through a fine sieve and leave to cool/coagulate completely.
Before using, mix to a smooth gel, eventually passing it through a very fine sieve.

STRAWBERRY-RASPBERRY CROQUANT

Ingredients
80 g isomalt sugar
20 g caster sugar
1 g xanthan gum (cold binder)
100 g fresh strawberries
100 g raspberry purée with 10% sugar
10 g glucose syrup
100 g white chocolate

Preparation
Mix the dry ingredients (isomalt, caster sugar, xanthan gum) and add to the strawberries, mixed with the raspberry purée and glucose syrup, in the Thermomix.
Heat to 50°C and then add the white chocolate and heat to 70°C. When this temperature is reached, the mix is heated at 70°C for 12 minutes.
Cover and leave to cool completely at 3°C.
Spread the mix thinly onto a silicone mat from the food drier and leave to dry for 6 hours at 65°C.

ALMOND GOLD

Ingredients
100 g almond shavings
75 g caster sugar
egg white

Preparation
Mix the shaved almonds with the caster sugar and add a little egg white until everything clings together. Press little quantities of the mix flat onto baking paper and bake golden brown at 160°C. When cool, rub in thinly a little gold powder (or spray with gold spray).

FINISHING
Little balls of watermelon
Strawberry pieces
Atsina cress, lime cress
Lemon verbena

CHAPTER 3

DESSERTS FOR PERSONS WITH FOOD SENSITIVITIES

All recipes, texts and info have been verified
and approved by a certified nutritionist.

Yoghurt – pistachio – cherry – almonds

Lactose-free

A lactose-free dessert with layers of soft yoghurt-pistachio-biscuit, cherry and almond cream.

YOGHURT-PISTACHIO BISCUIT

Ingredients
225 g eggs
225 g caster sugar
150 g lactose-free yoghurt
grated zest of ½ lemon
180 g flour
12 g baking powder
90 g almond powder 100%
90 g neutral oil (sunflower or grape seed oil)
90 g pistachio paste (pure)

Yield: enough for two 40 × 30 cm baking trays

Preparation
With the mixer, beat the eggs and caster sugar and then heat evenly to 38°C to obtain the desired foamy but sufficiently solid mass ('hot and cold' technique). Wait until the biscuit mass is cooler to the touch and then fold in the lactose-free yoghurt with the grated lemon zest. Using a spatula, fold in the pre-sieved mixture of flour, baking powder and almond powder. Stir the mixture of oil and pistachio paste into the biscuit. Spread out onto a baking tray with baking paper and bake for around 15 minutes at 180°C. After baking, immediately remove the biscuit from the baking tray.

SOUSING SYRUP

Ingredients
190 g water
10 g lemon juice
160 g caster sugar
½ vanilla stick
25 g Kirsch or Cointreau

Preparation
Bring the water and lemon juice to the boil together with the caster sugar and the cut-open, scraped (half) vanilla stick. Pour this through a fine sieve. Wait till the sugar syrup has cooled before adding the liqueur.

BOUND CHERRY COULIS

Ingredients
325 g cherry purée with 10% sugar
40 g caster sugar
42 g gelatine (or 3½ gelatine leaves)

Preparation
Heat the fruit purée with the sugar to 45°C and add the soaked gelatine. Spread the mixture 3 mm thick onto a Silpat baking mat and freeze for further preparation of the dessert.

ALMOND CRÈME

Ingredients
250 g almond paste, sprayable
260 g lactose-free milk
54 g gelatine (or 4½ gelatine leaves)
75 g almond milk (almond syrup – almonds and sugar only)
375 g lactose free-cream 36% fat, whippable

Preparation
Mix the almond paste and lactose-free milk to a homogeneous mass.
Mix this – step by step – with the already mixed mass of soaked gelatine and almond milk (40° C).
Mix again to a smooth mass.
At a temperature of 25°C, mix in the 2/3 whipped cream.

COMPOSING THE DESSERT

(building in a 4 cm high frame)
Place at the bottom the lightly soused biscuit, press onto it the pre-frozen cherry coulis and then spread a uniform layer (1 cm) of almond cream. Repeat this structure a second time in a frame so that the almond cream can be spread right up to the edge of the frame.
Cool sufficiently and then cut into 3 cm wide strips. Press three strips together (lay flat) by lightly brushing syrup (adhesive force) into the biscuit each time. Leave again to cool sufficiently. In this way the strips can be cut to the desired size (dessert on picture is 3 cm wide × 12 cm long and 3 cm high).

FINISHING

Spray the upper side with a thin layer of neutral glaze and cut to the desired size. Finish with some halved pistachios, cherries and a dash of lactose-free sweetened yoghurt with vanilla seeds.

Tangerine – coriander – grapefruit

Gluten-free – lactose-free – no added sugars

*Whether in adults or children, allergies are never fun!
Here therefore is a dessert with no added sugars, but also gluten and lactose-free!
Delicious mini-ice lollies with a fresh tangerine cream, a surprising sorbet of coriander, tangerine and lemon finished with pieces of white and pink grapefruit.*

FRESH TANGERINE CRÈME

Ingredients
200 g coconut oil
150 g egg yolks
140 g tangerine purée with 100% sugar
10 g of orange concentrate 100% (frozen)
120 g zusto

Preparation
Heat all ingredients to 82°C with the Thermomix for 15 minutes at setting 4. Then mix for another 10 seconds at setting 8 and cool to 35°C.
Place the crème half way up the small frisco moulds (until just under the opening of the stick) and freeze.

CORIANDER-TANGERINE SORBET WITH LEMON

Ingredients
20 g fresh coriander
555 g water
55 g fresh lemon juice
275 g zusto
combined stabilizer (emulsifier and stabilizer)
500 g tangerine purée with 100% sugar

Preparation
Briefly blanch the fresh coriander in hot water (90°C) and cool immediately in ice water.
Mix the blanched coriander finely in the cold water (555 g) with the lemon juice and mix it with the mixed dry ingredients (zusto and stabilizer).
Heat to 40° C and leave for half an hour to ensure optimal dissolving of the sugars and the gelling of the stabilizer. Only then add the tangerine pulp (3°C).
Churn the coriander-tangerine sorbet. Fill the half-filled frisco moulds to the top. Insert the stick and wipe flat. Freeze.

DIP MIX

Ingredients
120 g cocoa butter
120 g coconut oil
20 g yuzu oil
50 g zusto
yellow powder colouring (fat-soluble)

Preparation
Melt the cocoa butter and mix with the coconut oil, zusto and yuzu oil.
Mix in the desired amount of yellow powder colouring and pour through a fine sieve.
Immerse the ice lollies (-20° C) into the dip at 40°C.

/// CONSTRUCTION ///

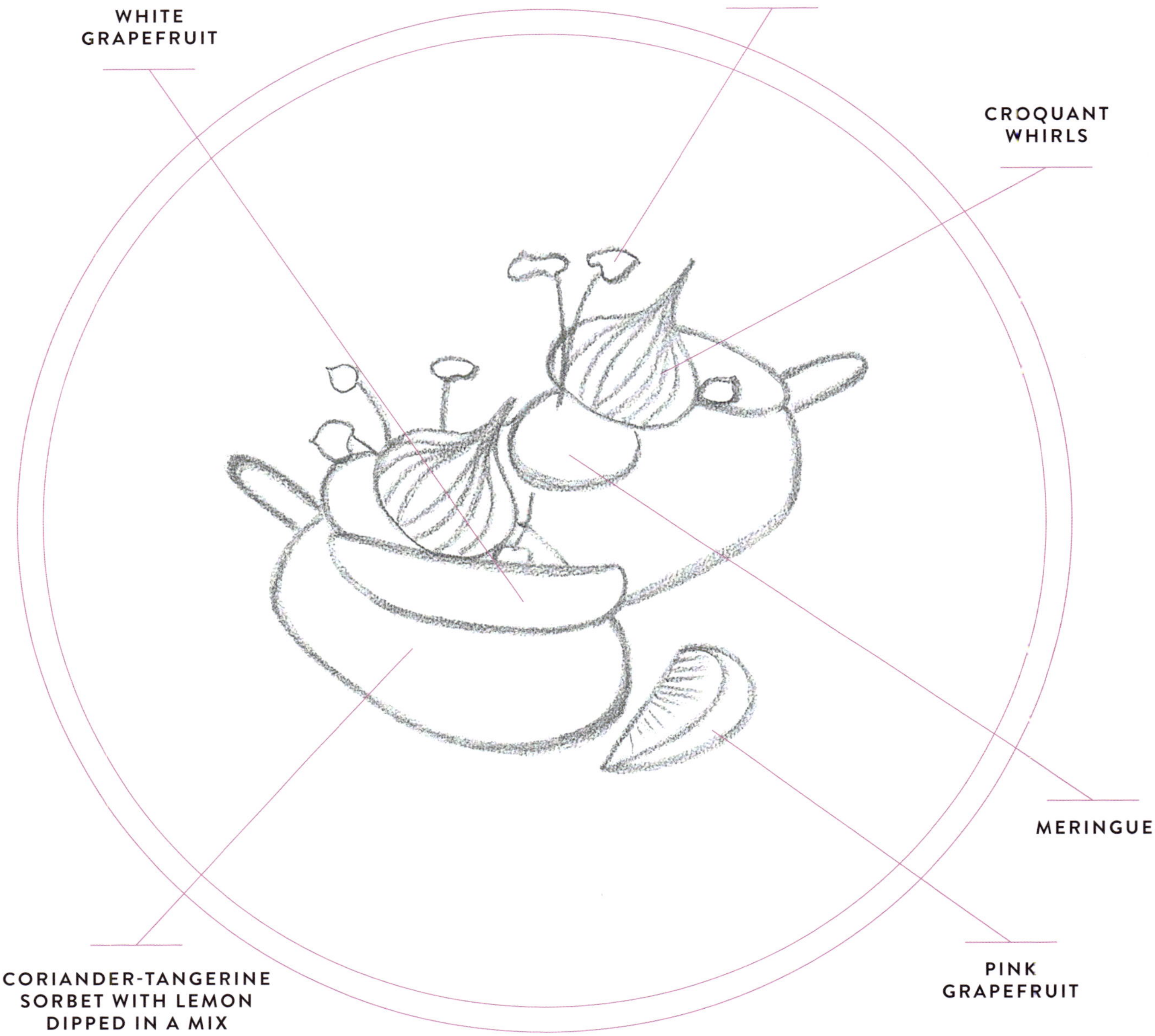

- WHITE GRAPEFRUIT
- ATSINA CRESS
- CROQUANT WHIRLS
- MERINGUE
- PINK GRAPEFRUIT
- CORIANDER-TANGERINE SORBET WITH LEMON DIPPED IN A MIX

- FRESH TANGERINE CRÈME
- CORIANDER-TANGERINE SORBET WITH LEMON

COOKING MERINGUE

Ingredients

175 g water
220 g zusto
220 g isomalt powder
220 g egg white

Preparation

Bring the water to the boil with the zusto and 210 grams of isomalt powder. Once the syrup boils, beat in the egg whites with 10 grams of isomalt powder (mixer on medium setting). Boil the syrup to 121°C. Then add in an even jet to the stiffly, but smoothly beaten egg whites.
Beat this cooking meringue at medium speed until cold.

PROCESSING ONTO CROQUANT WHIRLS

Using an icing bag with a toothed nozzle, spray soft meringue whirls onto a silicone mat from the food drier and leave to dry for 6 hours at 65°C.

FINISHING

Add some soft meringue together with some crispy whirls.
Use bits of white and pink grapefruit which has been 'peeled alive' (pelé à vif).
Atsina cress

WHY ZUSTO AS A SUGAR REPLACEMENT (SWEETENER)?

Zusto, used as a sugar substitute, consists of corn and chicory fibres, but as these lack the necessary sweetness, artificial sweeteners (usually sucralose) are added. In this way, the same sweetening value is obtained as with sucrose, making adaptations of recipes unnecessary. More importantly, the structural properties are almost identical to those of sugar (same final results in preparations and similar baking behaviour/properties).
Note: Fibres (zusto) dissolve more slowly in moisture and can therefore clot. To avoid this, the sweetener must be added more evenly to the preparation or mixed with other dry substances to ensure even absorption.

Chocolate – sansho – lemon

Gluten-free

A gluten-free dessert with a spicy chocolate crème, thanks to the spicy sansho, with a citrus accent. Very tasty in combination with a citrus crémeux, crispy chocolate-citrus crumble and unctuous coulis.

CHOCOLATE CRÈME WITH SANSHO

Ingredients
200 g whole milk
105 g cream (35%)
70 g egg yolks
30 g invert sugar
1 g sansho pepper
420 g fondant chocolate
440 g cream (35%)

Preparation
Prepare an anglaise of the first five ingredients by heating and stirring them together to 83°C. Then add through a sieve to the chocolate and mix to an emulsion (ganache). Wait till the mixture has cooled to 35°C and then mix in lightly the 2/3 whipped cream to give a slightly runny chocolate crème (reversed structure in Silpat baking moulds). After filling the moulds in the silicone mat – finish the chocolate crème with a thin slice of milk chocolate and praliné crunch.

CRUNCHY MILK CHOCOLATE AND PRALINÉ BASE

Ingredients
150 g milk chocolate
120 g hazelnut paste (50%)
    (50% half-roasted hazelnuts,
    50% caster sugar) (praliné)
75 g hazelnut paste 100%
45 g Crumiel (honey crystals – Texturas)
30 g popping sugar drops

Preparation
Mix the milk chocolate (40°C) with the two hazelnut pastes and add the Crumiel and popping sugar drops.
Roll out between baking paper sheets and press out circles of the desired size (slightly smaller than the silicone mould).

WHAT IS SANSHO PEPPER?
This Japanese-style pepper is a soft spicy pepper with a refreshing lemon flavour (a relative of the Chinese Szechuan pepper).

CHOCOLATE-CITRUS CRUMBLE

Ingredients
145 g butter
220 g caster sugar
grated zest of 4 oranges
grated zest of 1 lemon
220 g fine-ground hazelnut powder
180 gof chestnut flour (gluten-free flower)
40 g cocoa powder
5 g coarse sea salt

Preparation
Mix the butter (at room temperature) with the caster sugar, citrus zest and hazelnut powder. Then fold in the sieved mixture of gluten-free flour, cocoa powder and coarse sea salt to produce a homogeneous butter dough.
Crumble the butter dough on a baking tray lined with baking paper and bake at 150°C for 20-25 minutes. During baking, mix the crumble to give an evenly baked result.

/// CONSTRUCTION ///

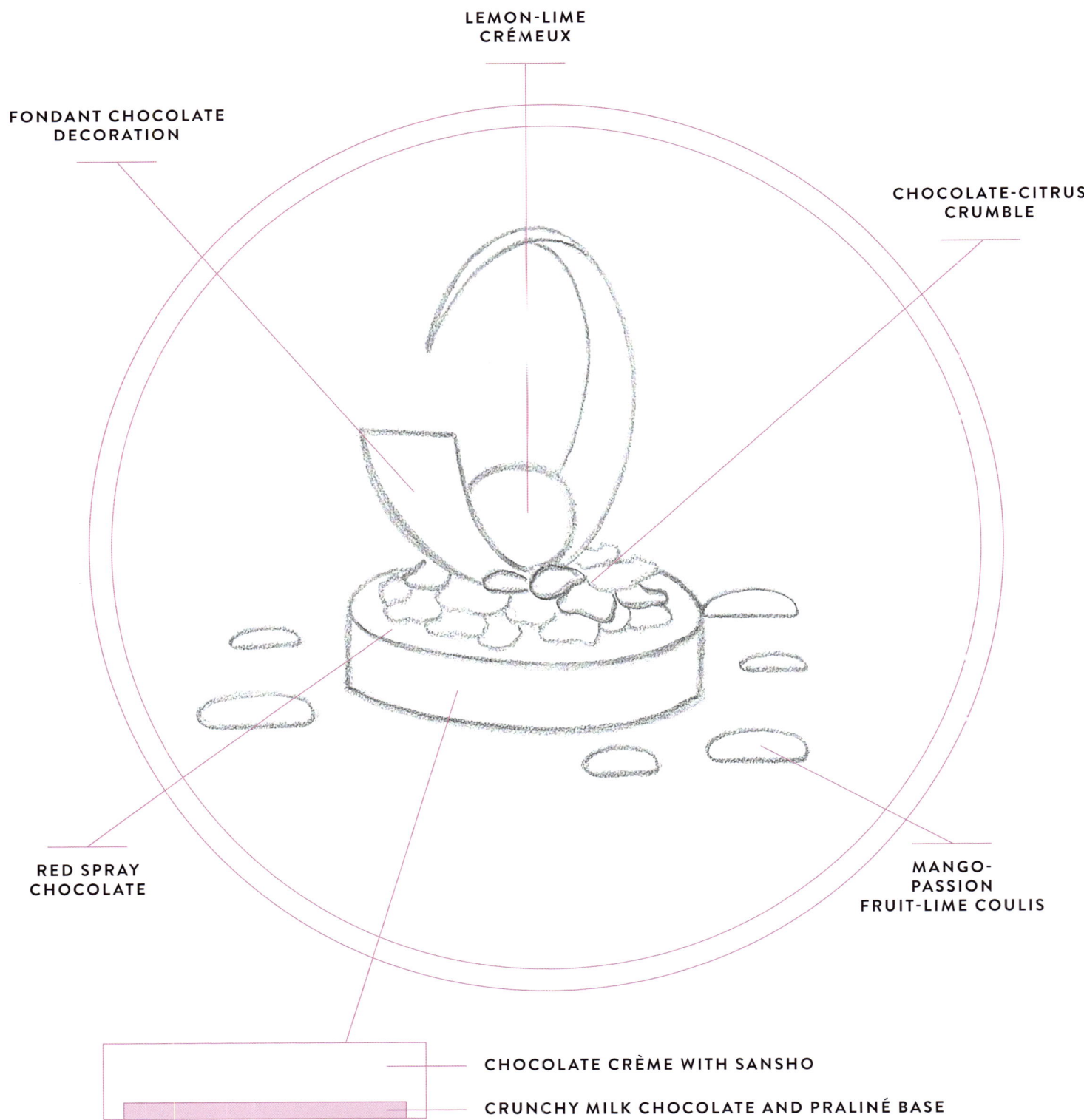

LEMON-LIME CRÉMEUX

Ingredients
125 g fresh lemon juice
125 g fresh lime juice
grated zest of 1 lime
150 g caster sugar
160 g eggs
140 g egg yolks
30 g gelatine (or 2½ gelatine leaves)
150 g butter

Preparation
Make an anglaise by heating and stirring the first six ingredients to 83°C, and then add the soaked gelatine. Allow to cool to 38°C before adding the soft butter to give a smooth emulsion (crémeux).
Place the crémeux into a 3D silicone ball mat and freeze for further use. Remove from the mould.
Glaze the resulting lemon-lime crémeux with a neutral jelly to which 5% lime juice (or else lime zest) and a few drops of yellow liquid colouring have been added.
Heat the glaze to 50°C to obtain an optimal, thin adhesion around the crémeux.

MANGO-PASSION FRUIT-LIME COULIS

Ingredients
135 g sugar syrup 1/1
230 g mango purée with 10 % sugar
150 g passion fruit purée with 10 % sugar
10 g lime juice
5 g mango vinegar
1 g xanthan gum (cold binder)

Preparation
Mix the sugar syrup with the fruit purée and the mango vinegar. Then mix briefly with the xanthan gum to obtain a somewhat thicker (not runny) coulis.

FINISHING
Spray the resulting pastry with spray chocolate (50% cocoa butter mixed with 50% fondant chocolate and a little red powder colouring) and cover with the chocolate-citrus crumble.
Finish with a decorative curl in fondant chocolate (chocolate decoration technique, see p. 31).
Place the glazed lemon-lime crémeux inside the chocolate curl.
Glaze the crémeux (ball) with neutral jelly flavoured with lime juice and a few drops of liquid yellow colouring. Heat the glaze to 50°C to obtain a thin layer round the crémeux.
Finish the edges of the pastry with dots of passion fruit-mango-lime coulis.

Pancake – chocolate – strawberries

Lactose-free with no added sugars

A delicious pancake with strawberries and chocolate sauce – it may look like a classic dessert, but this is one without added sugars and lactose-free!

PANCAKE BATTER

Ingredients
300 g eggs
35 g zusto or maltitol
500 g vegetal hazelnut milk
250 g flour
100 g fine-ground hazelnut powder
500 g vegetal almond milk
40 g vegetal fat

Preparation
Beat the eggs loosely with the sweetener and add the hazelnut milk and the flour alternately (to avoid clumping). Then add the hazelnut powder and lastly the warm milk with the molten vegetable fat. Mix the batter and pass through a sieve before baking.
Bake the batter in a hot pancake pan with little butter and toss the pancake half-way through baking.

CHOCOLATE SAUCE

Ingredients
250 g lactose-free milk
250 g lactose-free cream
300 g maltitol fondant chocolate

Preparation
Heat the lactose-free milk and cream to 50°C and add to the chocolate.
Mix the sauce to a homogeneous mass (emulsion). Cover and store at 3°C.
Reheat when serving the dessert.

SUGAR DECORATION: ISOMALT RINGS (SWEETENER)

For decorations on desserts, isomalt is used mainly in place of the classic water – sugar – glucose mix. Isomalt is easier and faster to use, there is no need to weigh it out, and the decorations, once made, are less sensitive to moisture absorption (much easier both to prepare and store).

Preparation and method
Melt the isomalt (no addition of moisture!) slowly until all grains have disappeared, then boil quickly to between 150 and 165°C. The hotter the cooking temperature, the better the shine and firmness and the less the sensitivity to moisture, but the more difficult to handle (need to work faster). If colouring is to be added, heat the isomalt to 130°C, add the colouring, and then heat further to 150-165°. Then add the desired liquid colouring and mix well.
As soon as it has reached the desired heat, pour the isomalt out onto a silicone mat. Regularly folding inwards the edges of the sweetener (using the silicone mat) produces a (colder) workable sweetener.

Now satinate by putting on sugar processing gloves and pulling the mass out and back together. During this process, the isomalt changes colour and the shine is created.

From now on keep the temperature of the isomalt stable by holding it under a sugar lamp. If it needs to be reheated at bit, use a microwave oven (put the sugar on a small silicone mat and heat briefly). Now make the uneven format isomalt decorative rings: draw out an end of the mass thinly but evenly and lay it round a cutting ring of the desired diameter. Cut the end of the still soft isomalt with good scissors.

Store the decorations in a sealed package, with layers of baking paper between the sugar decorations and with good 'moisture absorbers' for a good finishing.

FINISHING

Chopped strawberries inside the isomalt rings.

Blackcurrant – violet – red fruit

Lactose and gluten-free

*Fruity blackcurrant dessert with violets as a surprise addition!
The crumble, fruit croquant and marshmallow provide textural variety.*

BLACKCURRANT SORBET

Ingredients
400 g blackcurrant purée with 10% sugar
100 g raspberry purée with 10% sugar
310 g water
70 g violet sugar
45 g glucose powder
20 g dextrose
combined stabilizer (emulsifier and stabilizer)

Preparation
Mix the dry ingredients (violet sugar, glucose powder, dextrose and combined stabilizer) with the water and heat to 40°C. Leave for half an hour to ensure optimal dissolving of the sugars and gelling of the stabilizer. Only then add the mixed blackcurrant and raspberry purée (3°C) and churn.
Place at once into silicone 3D quenelle-shaped mats and freeze for further use.

VANILLA MARSHMALLOW

Ingredients
100 g water
280 g caster sugar
90 g invert sugar
125 g invert sugar
1 vanilla stick
72 g gelatine (or 6 gelatine leaves)

Preparation
Heat the water, caster sugar and the smallest amount of invert sugar to 114°C. Pour this sugar water onto the remaining invert sugar, the scraped-out vanilla stick and the soaked gelatine. Beat with a mechanical beater at medium speed into a light, frothy mass. Pour onto a silicone mat coated with icing sugar and spread out 15 mm thick. Sprinkle the top all over with icing sugar. Leave to harden overnight and then cut into even blocks of the desired size.
Keep dry in an airtight container.

VIOLET AND BLACKCURRANT BISCUIT

Ingredients
100 g isomalt
100 g violet sugar
1 g xanthan gum (cold binder)
200 g blackcurrant purée with 10% sugar
10 g glucose

Preparation
Mix all the dry ingredients (isomalt, violet sugar, xanthan gum) together and place in the Thermomix with the blackcurrant purée and glucose. Heat to 70°C and leave for 12 minutes at this temperature.
Cover and leave to cool completely at 3°C.
Before using, spread thinly onto a silicone mat from the food drier and leave to dry for 6 hours at 65°C (croquant).

/// CONSTRUCTION ///

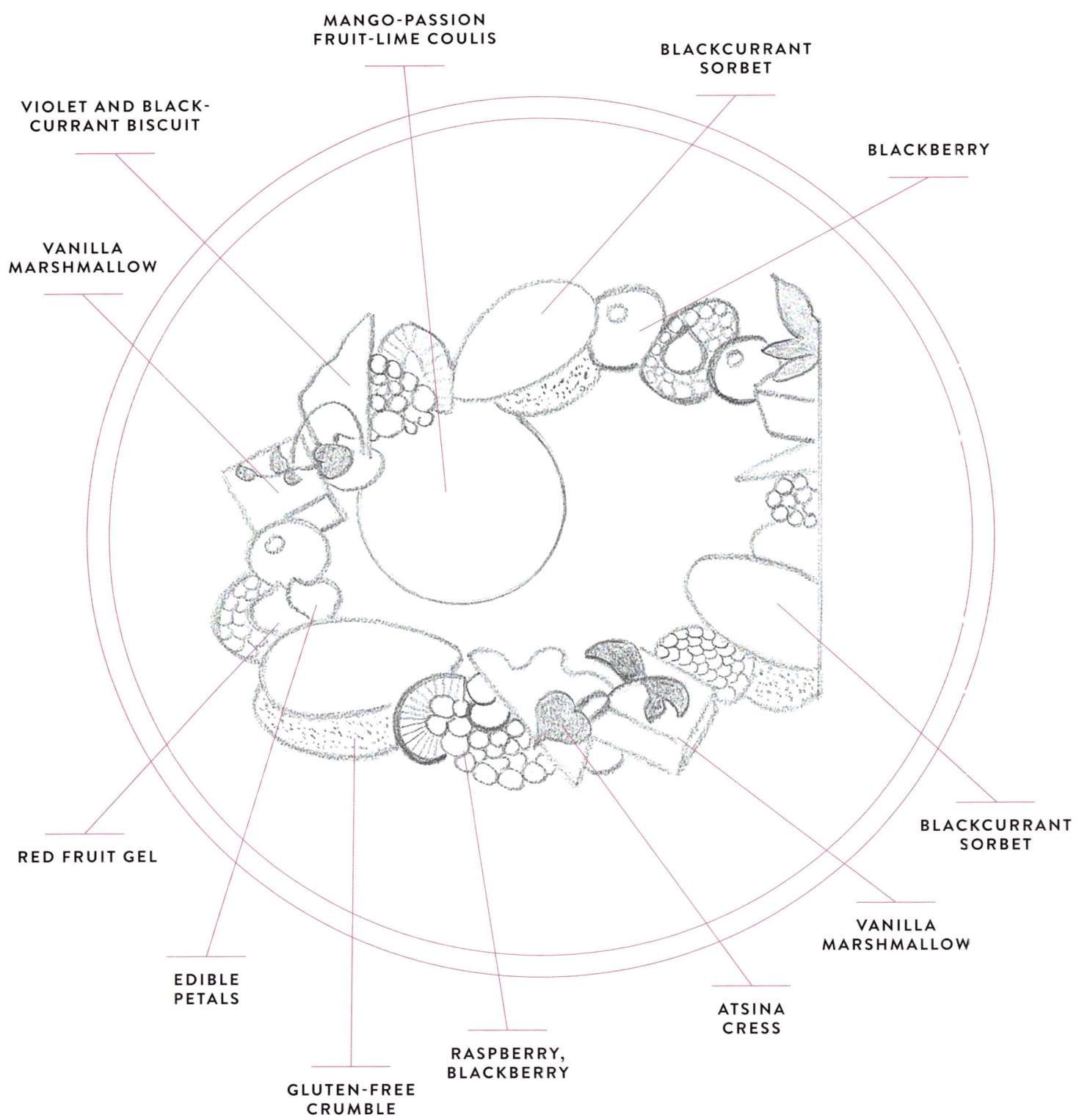

- MANGO-PASSION FRUIT-LIME COULIS
- BLACKCURRANT SORBET
- BLACKBERRY
- VIOLET AND BLACKCURRANT BISCUIT
- VANILLA MARSHMALLOW
- BLACKCURRANT SORBET
- VANILLA MARSHMALLOW
- ATSINA CRESS
- RASPBERRY, BLACKBERRY
- GLUTEN-FREE CRUMBLE
- EDIBLE PETALS
- RED FRUIT GEL

MANGO-PASSION FRUIT-LIME COULIS

Ingredients
135 g sugar syrup 1/1
230 g mango purée with 10% sugar
150 g passion fruit purée with 10% sugar
10 g lime juice
5 g mango vinegar
1 g xanthan gum (cold binder)

Preparation
Mix the sugar syrup with the fruit purée and the mango vinegar. Then mix briefly with the xanthan gum to obtain a somewhat thicker (not runny) coulis.

GLUTEN-FREE CRUMBLE

Ingredients
125 g vegetable fat
Grated zest of 1 orange
125 g caster sugar
110 g almond powder 100%
110 g gluten-free flour
2 g salt

Preparation
Mix the vegetable fat with the orange zest and caster sugar. Add the almond powder. Finally mix in the gluten-free flour with the salt to produce a homogeneous dough. Crumble on baking plates and bake at 150°C to a golden brown crumble. Once fully cooled, break up the crumble to the desired grain size.

RED FRUIT GEL
See p. 88

FINISHING
Assortment of red fruits (strawberry, raspberry, blackcurrant)
The fruit is lightly spiced with red fruit pepper (mix of pepper, coriander, aniseed, dried pieces of fruit, strawberry or blackberry)
Lime cress

A WORD OF HEARTFELT THANKS

- First and foremost to my wife Sandra and my daughter Silke for their unstinting support right through the project. You are both absolutely top!
- A big thank you also to my parents who always jumped into the breach when needed.
- To colleagues Christophe Declercq, Hans D'heer, Pol Deschepper and Peter Teerlinck, whose professionalism, enthusiasm, support and friendship I deeply appreciate!
- To certified dietician and colleague Kris Baeckelandt, for his willing and enthusiastic cooperation in expertly checking all the five desserts for food allergy sufferers – Essenweg 17, 8600 Diksmuide, www.krisbaeckelandt.be
- To friend and ceramicist Adina Laplasse (adinda.laplasse@telenet.be) for her support and the many made-to-measure plates.
- To photographer Kris Vlegels, for the many beautiful pictures and the pleasant professional cooperation during the shoots!
- To the managment and employees of Lannoc Publishers for the cooperation and trust.
- To the entire management of the Ter Groene Poorte gastronomy school and to the technical advisers of the bakery department for sponsorship and being allowed to use all kinds of equipment.

Spoorwegstraat 14
8200 Brugge
www.tergroenepoorte.be

SPECIAL THANKS TO:
- ISPC Gent, Ottergemsesteenweg Zuid 720, 9000 Gent, www.ispc.be
- N.V. Cnudde, Pontstraat 4, 8791 Beveren-leie, www.cnudde.com
- HVD Authentic Belgian waffle irons, Atomveldstraat 1 bus 2, 9450 Denderhoutem, www.hvd.be
- Kortrijkse zilvercentrale bvba, Sint-Anna 35, 8500 Kortrijk, www.nkz.be
- Point-virgule, Vaartlaan 9, 9800 Deinze, www.point-virgule.be
- Kenwood, Generaal de Wittelaan 17A/1, 2800 Mechelen, www.delonghigroup.com
- Chocolate world, Smallandlaan 4 unit 2, 2660 Antwerpen, www.chocolateworld.be
- Ranson NV, Generaal Deprezstraat 16, 8530 Harelbeke, www.ranson.be
- Gents bakkershuis, Drongensesteenweg 68, 9000 Gent, www.gentsbakkershuis.be
- Studio Mattes (stoneware – tableware), Steenweg 3, unit 16, 3540 Herk-de-Stad, www.studio-mattes.com

www.lannoo.com

Register on our web site and we will regularly send you a newsletter with information about new books and interesting, exclusive offers.

TEXT
Bart Ardijns

PHOTOGRAPHY
Kris Vlegels

ENGLISH TRANSLATION
Michael Lomax

GRAPHIC DESIGN
Leen Depooter – quod. voor de vorm.

If you have observations or questions, please contact our editorial office:
redactielifestyle@lannoo.com

©Uitgeverij Lannoo nv, Tielt, 2017
D/2017/45/592 – NUR 440
ISBN 978 94 014 4558 0

All rights reserved. Nothing from this publication may be copied, stored in an automated database and/or be made public in any form or in any way, either electronic, mechanical or in any other manner without the prior written consent of the publisher.